Walther Ziegler

Popper
in 60 Minutes

AF199423

Translated by
Alexander Reynolds

My thanks go to Rudolf Aichner for his tireless critical editing; Silke Ruthenberg for the fine graphics; Lydia Pointvogl, Eva Amberger, Christiane Hüttner, and Dr. Martin Engler for their excellent work as manuscript readers and sub-editors; Prof. Guntram Knapp, who first inspired me with enthusiasm for philosophy; and Angela Schumitz, who handled in the most professional manner, as chief editorial reader, the production of both the German and the English editions of this series of books.

My special thanks go to my translator

Dr Alexander Reynolds.

Himself a philosopher, he not only translated the original German text into English with great care and precision but also, in passages where this was required in order to ensure clear understanding, supplemented this text with certain formulations adapted specifically to the needs of English-language readers.

Bibliographic Information held by the German National Library: The details of the original German edition of this publication are held by the German National Library as part of the German National Bibliography; detailed bibliographical data can be found online at www.dnb.de.

1ˢᵗ Edition March 2020
Jacket design and graphic design for the whole book: Silke Ruthenberg, making use of illustrations by:
Raphael Bräsecke, Creactive – Studio for Advertising, Comics & Illustrations
© JackF - Fotolia.com (image-frames)
© Valerie Potapova - Fotolia.com (image-frames)
© Svetlana Gryankina - Fotolia.com (speech-balloons)

Publisher and Printing:
BoD – Books on Demand, Norderstedt
ISBN 978-3-7504-7089-7

Inhalt

Popper's Great Discovery   **7**

Popper's Central Idea   **24**

Popper's Revolutionary Theory of Knowledge:
Science as Merely Provisional Truth   24

Deduction Instead of Induction:
"A Human Being is not a Bucket"   31

Open and Closed Societies   39

The "Open Society" Instead of Plato's
"Government by the Best"   45

The False Prophets Hegel and Marx   58

Critical Rationalism as Constant Renewal
of Knowledge and Society   68

**Of What Use is Popper's Discovery
for Us Today?**   **73**

Popper's Notion of the
"Step-by-Step Improvement of Life"   73

Is Popper Right? Did Plato, Hegel and Marx
Prepare the Way for Totalitarianism?   77

The Positivism Dispute: Critical Rationalism
Instead of Critical Theory?   91

Popper's Legacy: All Life is Problem-Solving   99

Bibliographical References   **109**

Popper's Great Discovery

Karl Popper (1902-1994) is indisputably one of the truly great thinkers of the modern age. At once scholar of the natural sciences and philosopher of society, he has left a profound and decisive mark both on the theory of scientific knowledge and on our political and social self-understanding.

Born in Austria, he spent most of his professional life as a professor of philosophy in London, where he acquired, in 1949, British citizenship. In 1965 he was even knighted by the Queen. When Sir Karl Popper died at the age of 92 he was celebrated as "the philosopher of the 20th century" and as the last in the row of the great men of the Enlightenment. The key idea which was later to bring him world renown he developed already as a 17-year-old in the city of his birth, Vienna. He counts, indeed, along with Rousseau and a handful of others, as one of those exceptions among philosophers whose key notions suddenly come to them in perfect clarity, as a sort of epiphany or moment of sudden sublime insight, in their most tender years. Paradoxically, the moment of "illumination" in Popper's case was a moment of sudden darkness, namely, a solar eclipse:

We all – the small circle of students to which I belonged – were thrilled with the result of Eddington's eclipse observations which, in

1919, brought the first important confirmation of Einstein's theory of gravitation. It was a great experience for us, and one which had a lasting influence on my intellectual development.[2]

This solar eclipse of 1919 and the photographs taken of it by the British astronomer Eddington became, for Popper, a turning point in his life. Whereas he had been, up until then, a passionate adherent to the views of Newton, whose theory of gravitation he considered to be irrefutably true, he was now forced to entirely rethink his position. Because it was Eddington's photos of the positions of two particular stars that enabled Einstein to offer, for the very first time, real-world evidence of the truth of his revolutionary new theory of relativity.

In the celestial mechanics developed by Newton space is only a sort of receptacle which the various celestial bodies traverse, as time elapses, in perfectly straight lines. That a planet like Earth nonetheless takes a circular course around the sun is, according to Newton, due to the attraction of the "gravitational force" existing between sun and Earth. For Einstein, on the other hand, space and time are not independent magnitudes but rather blend together into a geometrical, four-dimensional continuum that Einstein referred to as "spacetime", this "spacetime" being the true cause of the curvature of the courses followed by all celestial bodies. The spacetime continuum, claimed Einstein, can even bend light and for this reason, he went on, it is possible to see in the night sky on certain days, such as the day of the eclipse on that 29th of May, stars which are in fact located far behind the sun and which ought, therefore, not to be visible. While the moon passes, for some minutes, directly in front of the sun and darkens the latter's brightness it is even possible to take photos of these stars. Through such photos, Einstein recognized, his theory of relativity would be either proven or disproven and Einstein even invited other researchers to proceed to such a real-world testing of his claims.

Though in that year of 1919 hostilities had barely ended between Germany and Great Britain, it was the latter country that mounted two expeditions to carry out this, the German physicist's wish. One of these was led by Eddington. And lo and behold, the photos taken by Eddington's expedition did indeed show the stars in question to be in positions that confirmed Einstein's hypothesis of a "curvature of spacetime" and not in those that they would, had the Newtonian gravitational theory held true, be expected to be in. Also according to this latter theory, indeed, the light of the stars in question would have succeeded in bypassing the sun; but this light would have been perceptible at quite other points and with a much smaller deviation.

In divergence from these Newtonian expectations, Einstein had predicted, on the basis of his idea of a curvature of spacetime, that the light-rays of the stars in question would undergo a deflection of 0.83 arc-seconds. And the measurements taken by Eddington turned out indeed to coincide astonishingly precisely with this prediction. This made Einstein a superstar of science overnight. The London *Times* headlined "Scientific Revolution. New Theory of the Universe. Newton's Conception Overthrown." The headline was no exaggeration because since Newton's founding, with his groundbreaking *Philosophiae Naturalis Principia Mathematica* of 1687, of classical mechanics and modern physics, everyone had believed that the key to the movement of physical bodies on the earth and the course of celestial bodies beyond it had once and for all been found. Now, however, the world in general, and Popper in particular, found they had to think again:

What is certain is that Einstein showed us that Newton [...] had to be corrected. And the Newtonian theory was, at that time, the best-proven, best-tested theory that there had ever been.[3]

If this is indeed the case, if even a genius like Newton could be wrong and his knowledge could have to be replaced after two hundred years by a better knowledge, then, so thought Popper, perhaps there are no such things as truths found "once and for all" at all. It was just at this point that Popper conceived his brilliant central idea:

> Scientific "knowledge" is not in fact knowledge; it is only *conjectural knowledge.*[4]

He formulates, indeed, this idea in still more radical terms:

> Even in the best and most certain science […] we have to do always only with supposed knowledge […] *Never with knowledge, always only with supposed knowledge.*[5]

The reason for this is not that Newton and other scientists did sloppy or methodologically imprecise work. It is rather a matter of the most basic and essential characteristics of the processes by which truth is discovered in the sciences. Popper's great discovery was that scientific knowledge consists, in principle, just in a series of ever-renewed hypotheses and models of explanation which count as true hypotheses and models only for so long as no counter-example, or no better model of explanation, has been found. With this discovery Popper placed in question the notion generally accepted by his contemporaries that scientific theories could be definitively proven by conducting series of experiments. Because, as Popper argued, even if a scientist succeeds in finding in the real world a thousand examples and proofs of the theory he is advancing, it is always possible that a counter-example will turn up and throw everything back into question. In his main work on the theory of the sciences, *The Logic of Scientific Discovery* of 1932, he illustrates this idea by the famous example of the swan:

No matter how many instances of white swans we may have observed, this does not justify the conclusion that *all* swans are white.[6]

Popper is referring here to an item of supposed knowledge that had been accepted for centuries. Swans had been known in Europe since earliest times and always as a large bird with white plumage. For centuries, therefore, the sentence "all swans are white" had counted as an example of evident truth. When Europeans first came to Australia, however, they were amazed to discover a type of swan with black plumage. That long-established textbook example of a true proposition to the effect that "all swans are white" was suddenly proven to be false or, as Popper puts it, was "falsified".

"Falsification", indeed, is the concept that is key to understanding of Popper's theory of science. Scientific progress, so runs his provocative thesis, does not rest, as so many of his contemporaries believed it did, on induction: i.e. on the logical derivation of regularities from knowledge acquired by experiment. On the contrary, it rests on theoretical hypotheses and on these latter's "falsification" once they have been advanced. As soon as a hypothesis has been proven false by the emergence of a counter-example to whatever it advances, it must be replaced by a new and better hypothesis – a process which leads us, over the long term, closer and closer to truth. This process of drawing ever closer is the core and the essence of scientific progress.

We may predict, with Popper, that even Einstein's much-celebrated theory of relativity will count as true only until some better explanatory model is discovered. And where does this end? Might we arrive after all, even if only in ten or a hundred thousand years, at some final certainty, some definitive and absolute truth? Popper's answer here is a sobering one. He cites the Pre-Socratic philosopher Xenophanes:

But as for certain truth, no man has known it; nor will he know it [...] For all is but a woven web of guesses.[7]

In a newspaper interview given toward the end of his life, Popper confessed:

Science is indeed something wonderful. All the same, we know nothing [...] Scientific progress consists [...] in discovering errors and replacing them with something better: namely, with a better hypothesis.[8]

There can and will, then, never be anything but an approximation to the truth. Since space and time are infinite, we human beings can never fully measure, let alone explain, the infinite dimensions of the universe. We do, however, continue constantly to draw closer to the truth. Our "guesses" become, as time goes on, better and better:

> We know, for example, that the Ptolemaic system, the Ptolemaic interpretation of the solar system which takes the earth to be at its centre, is less good, less close to the truth than is the heliocentric system of Aristarchus, Copernicus and Kepler.[9]

"Helios" is the Greek word for "sun". In the heliocentric world-picture the earth circles the sun, something which comes closer to the truth than does the Ptolemaic assumption that the earth itself forms the absolute centre point of everything. Precisely because we human beings are capable of drawing ever closer to the truth, and indeed have to do so, it is of the very greatest importance that society remains open to the possibility of calling knowledge into question. Here, then, Popper adds to and completes that core idea of his which we have cited above:

[...] If we wish to remain human, then there is only one way: the way into the open society.[10]

By "open society" Popper means a society such as permits, at any time, the free expression of opinion, criticism, falsifications, and new scientific hypotheses. A counter-example to such a society, or in other words an example of a "closed society", would be the theocratic state presided over by Pope Urban VIII. This was the 17th-century theocratic state which refused, in obedience to its own religious dogmas, to accept Galileo's discovery of the movement of the planets around the sun and even took steps to suppress this discovery. Galileo, famously, was forced under threat of torture to recant his theories in court of law since, so it was insisted, God alone determined the course of the planets and God's plans for Man lay beyond the purview of human reason.

It is just such dogmatism as this that Popper refuses and rejects. Scientific research requires an open society if it is ever to lead to a real improvement in human knowledge. Nor, moreover, are there any truths established "once and for all" in the sphere of politics. Also those sociological and economic hypotheses on which the measures taken by governments are based must be such as to be susceptible of falsification, that is, such that they prove sometimes to be bad and to have to be replaced by better ones. It must also be possible for every citizen to criticize and influence these policies followed by their governments. But how exactly should one go about critically supervising governments and falsifying the measures they employ? Popper himself poses this important question:

How can one keep a government under enough pressure to prevent it from doing anything excessively bad? The answer to this is simply: by ensuring that it is a government one can remove.[11]

Popper's central idea, then, of knowledge as never more than "conjectural knowledge" leads naturally to a plea in favour of democracy. Only a democracy, with free elections, free expression of opinion, freedom of the press and the guarantee of further basic rights can ensure the necessary regular renewal of natural-scientific and socio-political knowledge. But the "open society" is in constant danger, threatened by totalitarian systems such as National Socialism, communism and religious fundamentalism. Popper came from a Jewish family and lost fourteen of his relatives during the Holocaust. He himself was able to emigrate, just in time, with his immediate family from Austria to New Zealand. It was there that he wrote his masterpiece of social-political analysis *The Open Society and Its Enemies*:

[I took] the final decision to write [this book] in March 1938, on the day I received the news of [Hitler's] invasion of Austria.[12]

The first volume of this book, which is five hundred pages long just in itself, bears the title *The Open Soci-*

ety and Its Enemies: The Spell of Plato. The title is some-
what misleading. It ought really to be called *The False
Spell of Plato,* since Popper strongly criticizes Plato in
this book as a thinker who seduced his readers down
dangerous roads and paved the way for dictatorship:

He was a magician – not,
admittedly, one like Hitler but
one who resembled certain
other highly gifted men whom
I find, nonetheless, morally
unacceptable.[13]

Plato, argues Popper, cast a spell over many generations of readers with his doctrine of the Ideas of the
Good, the True and the Beautiful and of the immor-
tality of the soul while all along, behind this spell-
binding façade, promoting a vision that led inevitably to dictatorship and concentration camps. Plato,
Popper contended, was an enemy of the open society:

> He wanted to introduce a dictatorship of his own Platonic philosophy and in the great work of his old age, *The Laws*, he explains how those

> whose way of thinking is contrary to this philosophy should be held in solitary confinement and, if they do not recant, should be put to death.[14]

The "false prophets Hegel and Marx", Popper went on, had proceeded differently from Plato but in a way no less conducive to totalitarianism. They had paved the way for our modern dictatorships by prescribing for human beings a "goal of history" which, they said, had to be reached at all costs:

> Marx's historical claim that socialism had to come sooner or later was an immensely influential one […] It led to the even more fateful formulation […] that those who refuse socialism are committing a serious crime.[15]

Where history, as by Hegel and Marx, is predicted to have a specific end or goal, this must automatically mean an end to the open society. Because, as Popper points out, in the face of such a firm prediction it is impossible any longer to criticize or alter society's further development. Every suggestion, idea or action is now measured solely by the criterion of whether or not it serves the final goal: in Marxism's case, for example, the classless society. For this reason Popper gave to the second volume of his social-philosophical masterpiece, which focused on Hegel and Marx, the title: *The High Tide of Prophecy*. And against these two German philosophers, as already against Plato, he levels an extremely serious reproach:

The ideology of Nazism would have been impossible if German philosophers had known some intellectual responsibility.[16]

Instead of attempts to achieve lofty historical-philosophical goals Popper calls on us rather to pursue a politics of "small steps" and, if we must practice "social engineering", to let it be only a "piecemeal social engineering". It is time, he argues, to finally apply to politics the natural-scientific methodology of trial and error, hypothesis and falsification.

Is Popper right? Is all our knowledge just a matter of conjecture, resting only on trial and error? Did Plato, Hegel and Marx really prepare the way, with their ideas, for totalitarianism? Must we really learn to take, in future, no longer such visions as those of these philosophers but rather the scientific method of trial and error as our compass in the improvement of society? And: is it really possible to solve the problems that face us by means of an only "piecemeal" style of social engineering? Popper gives clear and unmistakable answers to all these questions.

Popper's Central Idea

Popper's Revolutionary Theory of Knowledge: Science as Merely Provisional Truth

Popper's central philosophical idea, whereby all our knowledge is merely provisional, i.e. a "conjectural knowledge" which is subject at any time to alteration, represented, at the time he first advanced it, an enormous provocation. Before Popper, researchers and scientists had generally believed that there really were such things as "laws of Nature", i.e. ultimate laws to which the cosmos had to conform and which determined all that happened in it. A generation as recent as that of our own grandfathers still learnt from their physics teachers that these "laws of Nature", in contradistinction to the claims of religion and mere belief, represented authentic knowledge. Now that the secrets of these laws had been unlocked by science, and most particularly by the theories of mechanics and gravitation developed by Newton, one was in a position, or such was the suggestion, to understand the world once and for all and to solve all the problems posed by it. Newton's theory appeared to be the crown and completion of all science:

Here was real knowledge; knowledge beyond the wildest dreams of even the boldest minds. Here was a theory that explained precisely not only the

movements of *all* the stars in their courses but also, just as precisely, the movements of bodies on earth, such as falling apples, or projectiles, or pendulum clocks. And it even explained the tides.[17]

This mood of enormous confidence was in fact typical of that age of the Industrial Revolution that set in around a hundred years after Newton's remarkable discoveries and largely on the basis of these. Humanity's belief in progress was still unconditional. Almost daily, some new discovery, invention or machine came along to further revolutionize everyday life. Liebig's fertilizers multiplied the yields of agriculture; Arkwright's new spinning frames and Cart-wright's looms saw to it that whole populations, for the first time in history, were properly clothed. Iron began, on a large scale, to be successfully smelted from iron ore and soon the whole world witnessed how even the most distant locations could be bound together by railways and by steamships.

Newton's mechanics and theory of gravitation, along with their practical implementation in technical revolutions, appeared to have explained the whole of Nature and subjected it once and for all to Man's control. Faith in progress and euphoria over the new techniques were so strong at this time that the British manufacturer of steel goods Wilkinson had himself buried in a steel coffin under a three-foot-high steel obelisk. Nature's laws had finally been revealed, so that everything now seemed possible. With Newton's physics, it was generally believed, Man had climbed to the very summit and endpoint of all possible knowledge. Until, that is, that solar eclipse of 1919.

With Einstein, and the conclusions that Popper drew from Einstein's 1919 vindication, this euphoria and this illusion came suddenly to an end. Nature itself, Popper now declared to the world, knows no laws. Rather, it is Man who imputes laws to Nature. It is a kind of hubris, then, to speak of "laws of Nature" at all. What were long called "laws of Nature", Popper went on, were really only products of the minds of certain scientists which had been applied to Nature, sometimes with more success and sometimes with less. It is we human beings, then, not Nature, that make these "laws". And we, being fallible, make mistakes as we do so and must, again and again, correct these mistakes:

My theory of science, then, is terribly simple. It is *us* who create scientific theories and also us who critique these theories [...] *We* invent the theories and *we* kill our own theories off.[18]

It is necessary, then, to draw a clear distinction between the inventing of theories and the actual physical world. The physical world of Nature, argues Popper, exists completely independently of the human mind and is something of a radically different kind from Man's experience of it. And just because this is so we must always adopt a critical attitude toward all the theories into which we attempt to cram Nature and must remain mistrustful of our own supposed knowledge. Nature and mind can never be brought into total harmony with one another. The scientist, therefore, must be aware, each time he arrives at some new piece of knowledge, that this latter will remain valid only until some new knowledge comes along to refute and invalidate it. Were researchers completely serious about their work, each one of them would attempt, before publishing his or her theory, to prove this latter false and, in the case where this attempt proved successful, drop the theory again, unpublished. In this regard, Popper considered Einstein to be the model of the true scientist:

Einstein, for example, writes [...] that during the ten, fifteen years that he was working on the general theory of relativity he found himself scrapping a theory he'd come up with about once every three minutes.[19]

Moreover, Einstein himself had, just prior to the great eclipse of 1919 that had been such a turning point for Popper, personally urged other scientists to test those predictions of his ensuing from the theory of relativity and, if possible, to prove them false and reject them:

> [...] What impressed me most was Einstein's own clear statement that he would regard his theory as untenable if it should fail in certain tests.[20]

With this invitation to falsify his theory, Einstein ran the greatest imaginable risk, yet remained very modest while doing so:

> Einstein was looking for crucial experiments whose agreement with his predictions would by no means establish his theory; while a disagreement, as he was the first to stress, would show his theory to be untenable.[21]

It was this attitude that led Popper to the really decisive idea for his theory of scientific knowledge. If the very best that could be hoped for, as regards Einstein's theory, from these photographs taken during the eclipse of 1919 was not that this theory would thereby be proven true for all time but only that it would remain, for the present at least, un-disproven, then it followed that the decisive criterion for the truth or otherwise of a scientific claim was not, as had hitherto generally been believed, the successful performance of a large number of experiments that would go to confirm the claim in question but rather the disconfirmation of this claim which might occur through one single experimental finding. Or, to recur to the "swan" example alluded to above: not even a thousand successive photos of white swans can finally and definitively confirm the claim that "all swans are white"; but if, on taking a thousand-and-first photo, the swan shown on it proved to be black, this would indeed finally and definitively disconfirm this claim or, to use Popper's terminology, definitively "falsify" the "all swans are white" theory:

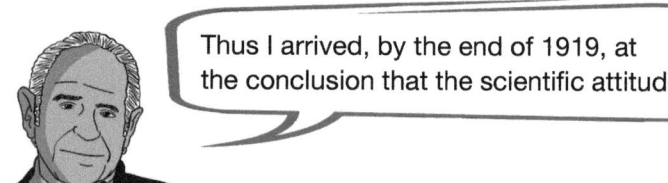

Thus I arrived, by the end of 1919, at the conclusion that the scientific attitude

was the critical attitude, which did not look for verifications but for crucial tests: tests which could refute the theory tested, though they could never establish it.[22]

In this way Popper's new theory of science was born. Popper put falsification in the place of verification. But this was not all he did. He also posed the question of how scientists arrived at their theories in the first place.

Deduction Instead of Induction: "A Human Being is not a Bucket"

How do scientific theories arise? At the time of Popper's first writing the inductive method was the most generally adopted and recognized practice. Popper himself, though, was a passionate advocate of the deductive method, arguing that it was an epistemological approach that was both more honest and yielded richer results.

"Induction" comes from the Latin word *inducere*, meaning "lead into" or "take up into". To follow the "inductive method", then, implies that one must first "take up" or gather into oneself a large number of sense-impressions and experiences in order subsequently, in a second step, to form, from all these gathered-up impressions and experiences, a theory. Popper rejects this account of theory-formation, calling it "the bucket theory of the human mind". He mockingly writes of the inductive theory that, for this latter

Our head is a bucket. The bucket has holes in it and through these holes there flows information about the world.[23]

In this "allegory of the bucket", then, our eye-sockets and the openings of our ears and nose would be the "holes" through which images, sounds, smells and other empirical impressions would enter into us. Scientists proceeding according to the inductive method look for some common denominator for these impressions; that is to say, they try to formulate theoretical statements which can apply equally and universally to all these empirical experiences that come seeping into our consciousness:

For many people believe that the truth of these universal statements is *'known by experience'*. [24]

According to this "bucket theory", through the evaluation of the maximum quantity of data taken up and gathered into oneself in this way one should, in the end, be able to arrive at a fully secured and established knowledge. But it is just such a procedure that Popper calls fundamentally into question:

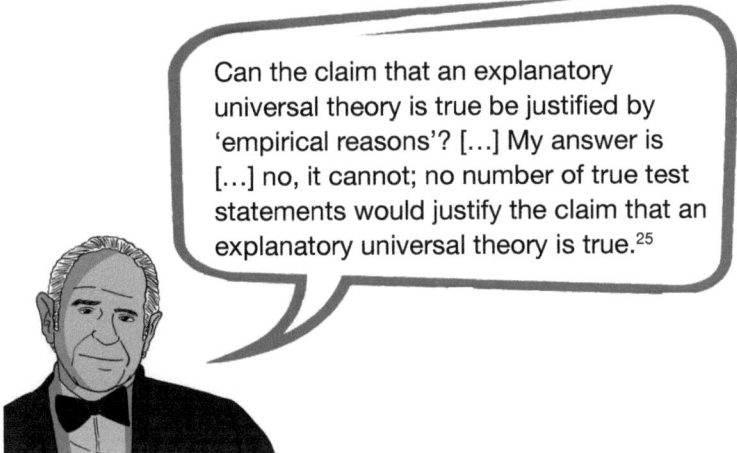

Can the claim that an explanatory universal theory is true be justified by 'empirical reasons'? [...] My answer is [...] no, it cannot; no number of true test statements would justify the claim that an explanatory universal theory is true.[25]

Here, the swans enter once again into the question. No number of test statements about swans can possibly confirm the truth of the "all swans are white" theory. As Popper points out, if one wished really definitively to prove a proposition like "all swans are white" using the inductive method, one would have to be able to put "into the bucket" all swans living, dead and not yet born, without exception. But this is clearly impossible in basic principle:

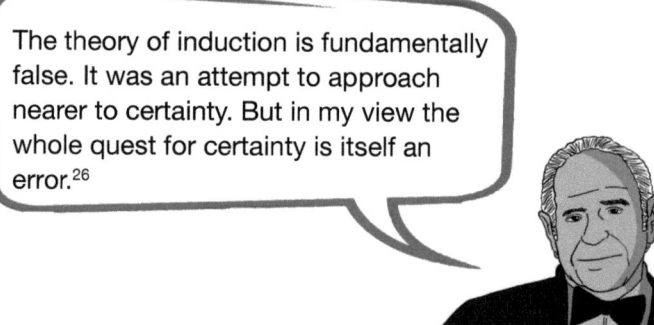

The theory of induction is fundamentally false. It was an attempt to approach nearer to certainty. But in my view the whole quest for certainty is itself an error.[26]

There also speaks against the "bucket theory" and its notion of science as a vast gathering of experiential data the fact that the certainties acquired are always necessarily subjective. For example, the experience that we have every day of light returning at dawn may well lead us to set up as a universal proposition: "at the end of every night the sun rises". The knowledge expressed in this proposition can prove practically very useful in everyday life and may, for example, when combined with other experiences, contribute to the writing of an almanac. From a broad cosmological viewpoint, however, the proposition is false.

Because for other planets this rhythmical shift from night to day may not apply, any more than any other information contained in an earth-related almanac. This is why, for Popper, the inductive method is, quite generally speaking, a "dead end" for the theory of knowledge. In the final analysis, the human brain, and the science that emerges from it, are anything but "buckets":

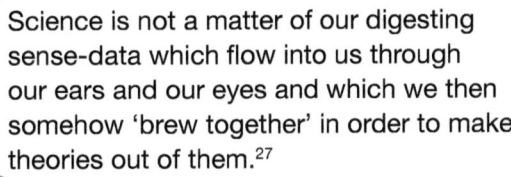

Science is not a matter of our digesting sense-data which flow into us through our ears and our eyes and which we then somehow 'brew together' in order to make theories out of them.[27]

It is, in fact, the very reverse of this that is the case. In its fundamental essence science is something bold and active:

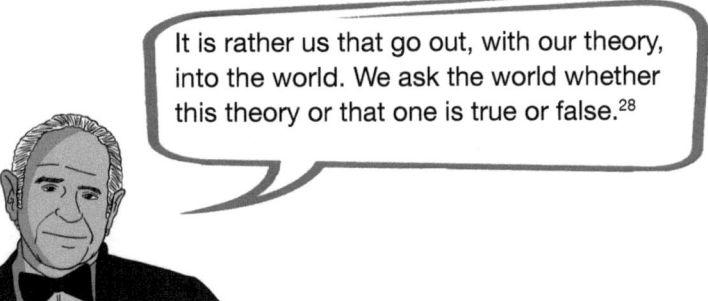

It is rather us that go out, with our theory, into the world. We ask the world whether this theory or that one is true or false.[28]

And this means:

There is only activity – an active seeking for laws – and the forming of theories. And there is also a process of selection among theories. That, in short, is my whole philosophy of knowledge.[29]

Science, then, is, in the first instance, characterized by imaginativeness and invention. Only as a second step in the scientific process are the theories invented tested as regards their applicability to the real world. Science is thereby based on a process of "trial and error". Popper's great plea in favour of the deductive, rather than inductive, method is founded on this insight. "Deduction" comes from the Latin word *deducere* meaning "lead out from" or "derive from". This means that we first form the theory and then, in a second step, derive from it the results which are to be expected. Only at the end of this process do we look to the real physical world to see whether we have gotten things right or are in error:

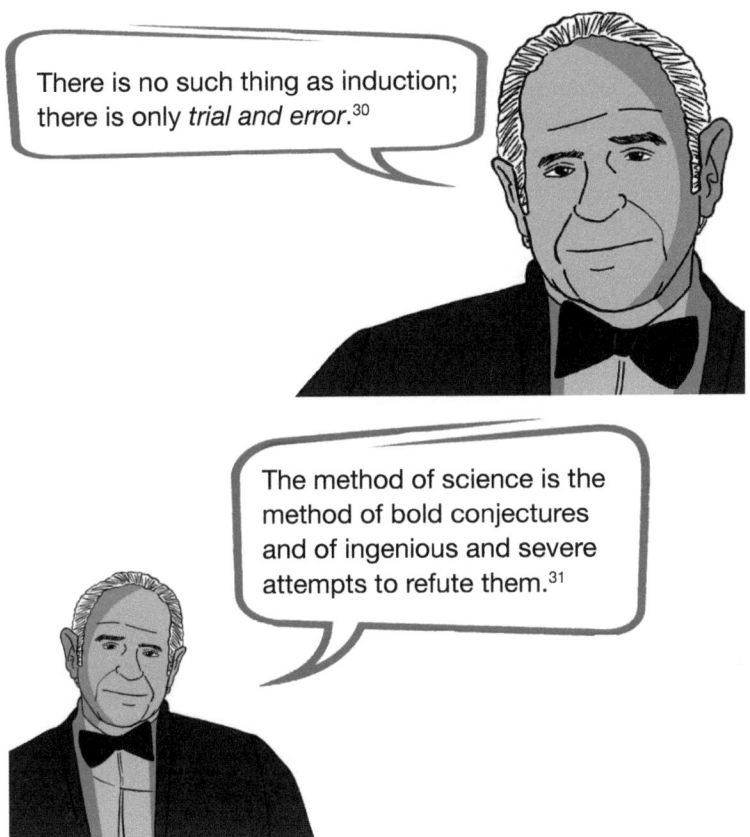

There is no such thing as induction; there is only *trial and error*.[30]

The method of science is the method of bold conjectures and of ingenious and severe attempts to refute them.[31]

Popper points out that Einstein too had practiced the deductive method. Einstein himself had written: "Only bold speculation can bring us forward, not the mere gathering of facts." Interestingly, Popper even raised the demand that the deductive method be used in the teaching of the sciences to schoolchildren. Popper saw, in his own day, children still being taught in ways aligned with the inductive "bucket theory":

A funnel is specially added to the bucket and into this funnel knowledge is poured [...] The children are overloaded with answers before they have themselves posed any questions.[32]

It is important however, Popper argues, that we encourage our children too to proceed in line with the deductive method and pose bold questions, develop their own theories, and look for answers using the "trial and error" procedure. Children, of course, would inevitably encounter many failures here but precisely this would teach them to think for themselves.

To sum up, then: both the free unfolding of children's personalities and the continuing development of science require the advancing of ever new hypotheses and conjectures and also the refutation of these latter. From this central idea Popper goes on to derive a further, highly important socio-political conclusion. If new hypotheses are really to have a chance there is also needed what Popper calls an "open society".

Open and Closed Societies

This idea of an "open society" is the notion on which Popper's whole political philosophy turns. It is at the same time an ideal and an actually existing historical phenomenon. The "open society" is, on the one hand, something that the Ancient Greeks succeeded in actually implementing and it exists, indeed, even today in many modern states; on the other hand, it is a theoretical ideal. Popper himself defines this, his key political-philosophical concept, in the following way:

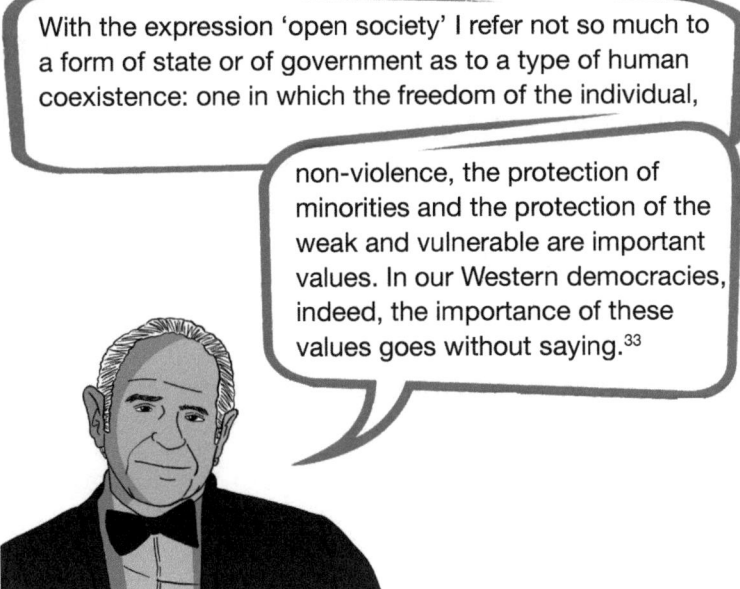

With the expression 'open society' I refer not so much to a form of state or of government as to a type of human coexistence: one in which the freedom of the individual, non-violence, the protection of minorities and the protection of the weak and vulnerable are important values. In our Western democracies, indeed, the importance of these values goes without saying.[33]

When one considers human historical development as a whole, however, the open society is something that makes its appearance only very late. Originally, Popper contends, the whole world consisted only of closed societies. Human beings all lived tightly bound into their clans, into nomadic hordes, or into other forms of tribally-based societies:

It is one of the characteristics of [...] a primitive tribal or 'closed' society that it lives in a charmed circle of unchanging taboos, [...] laws and customs [...].[34]

In such societies each member had to do what the chief ordered or what was prescribed by custom or ritual. And each one also was born into a position within the fixed hierarchy of the tribe: i.e. as chief, shaman, warrior, hunter, farmer, servant or slave. In the place of any rational justification for one man's exercising power rather than another there ruled myths of family origin: for example, the story that a certain chief was descended from the sun god and thus himself a deity, so that he had to be revered by all. Individuality played no role in such societies:

Based upon the collective tribal tradition, the institutions leave no room for personal responsibility.[35]

As an example of such a collectivistically organized, tribally-based society Popper mentions the Ancient Greek warrior state Sparta, which was indeed, in comparison for example to the Athenian democracy under Pericles, extremely authoritarian and collectivistic:

A closed society (is) a semi-organic unit whose members are held together by [...] kinship, living together, sharing common efforts, common dangers, common joys and common distress.[36]

Thus the Spartans, for example, felt themselves to form, under their famous King Leonidas, a proud community of shared blood and a mutually solidary collective that needed to defend and assert itself, even at the cost of great sacrifices, against other

Greek city-states and foreign powers like the Persians. Also in the Middle Ages almost every existing society was, where we adopt Popper's definition of the term, a "closed society": in this case "closed societies" that were governed by noblemen and clerics according to certain religious and mythical rules and values. The cardinals, bishops and priests spoke no other language but Latin together and enjoyed sole disposal over the knowledge, which was also a form of power, which enabled them to explain the Bible to the common people and to dictate the duties of religious life. The noblemen, for their part, were seen as rulers "by birth", entitled to govern by their "blue blood".

Such things as the citizen's personal responsibility for his or her own life, the possibility of personal social mobility, and shared responsibility for the welfare of society as a whole come into being only with the coming into being of the "open societies" of the modern era, also called democracies:

The transition takes place when social institutions are first [...] recognized as man-made and when their conscious alteration is discussed [...].[37]

In the open society governments and parliaments are institutions that can be criticized; indeed they are institutions that are called into existence by the citizens themselves and that can, therefore, be voted out of power. Popper celebrates the transition from the closed to the open society as "the birth of civilization" and "the greatest revolution in history":

[...] The greatest of all moral and spiritual revolutions of history [...] is the longing of uncounted unknown men to free themselves [...] from the tutelage of authority and prejudice.[38]

[...] It is their attempt to build up an open society.[39]

Today, we enjoy, in many modern states, the fruits of this centuries-long struggle for self-determination. We have free elections, free choice of profession, freedom of speech and expression and can, in all respects, fashion our individual lives the way we please. But such an unconstrained life in an open society also has its price. If, for example, we live in a huge anonymous metropolis and earn our living working alone at home on the computer, performing a job from which we feel utterly alienated, this can lead to profound feelings of loneliness and isolation. The old "extended family" structures that existed in past centuries are now mostly dissolved and also the psychological shelter once provided by such local religious institutions as the "parish" is, for most people, a thing of the past. The great danger now, Popper points out, is that people will begin to feel a longing for the shelter and security that tribally-based societies had once offered. But a return to such societies, Popper insists, is impossible or rather, were we to attempt it, the attempt would turn us into "beasts":

> We can never return to the alleged innocence and beauty of the closed society [...] *There is no return to a harmonious state of Nature. If we turn back, then we must go the whole way – we must return to the beasts.*[40]

Thus, Popper understood National Socialism, for example, as a dangerous lapse back into the bestiality of tribally-based society. Nazism was, for Popper, an example of the attempt to set up a closed society which drew its legitimacy from "shared blood", a "community of the nation" and a collective struggle against other tribes and races. In the light of this terrible example, it is imperative that we remain vigilant and hold high the ideals of the open society:

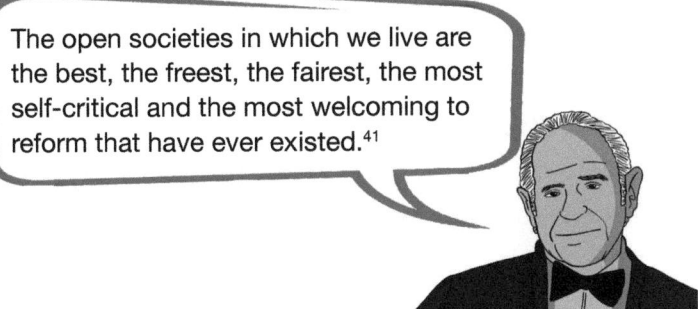

The open societies in which we live are the best, the freest, the fairest, the most self-critical and the most welcoming to reform that have ever existed.[41]

The "Open Society" Instead of Plato's "Government by the Best"

Popper's commitment was fed from two key sources. On the one hand, from his recognition of the fact that society must, in principle, be open to new hypotheses and falsifications if science and technology are going to go on being improved. On the other hand, however, from his own painful personal experience of what inhumane consequences for human beings result from closed societies such as National Socialism or communism.

Popper himself spent the Second World War in exile in New Zealand. But as a native of Austria he was horrified to see what went on in his native country during those years.

Raised in the great liberal-minded metropolis Vienna, where he had maintained, as a young man, a lively intellectual exchange with Carnap and other members of the Vienna Circle, Freudian psychoanalysts such as Adler and other intellectuals, it initially seemed to him incomprehensible how countries like Austria and Germany could lapse back into the barbarism of National Socialism.

The values of the Enlightenment, he was forced to recognize, were rapidly abandoned not only by the general populations of these countries but also by their intellectual elites. This prompted him to pose a question of enormous consequence: what attitude of mind, doubtless inherited from immediately preceding generations but with possibly very deep historical roots, had made such a fall back into barbarism possible?

> I set about searching for clues, then, all the way through history, from Hitler back to Plato, the first great political ideologue to think in terms of classes and races and to propose the establishment of concentration camps.[42]

Even the famous classical philosopher Plato, then, so argued Popper, could be seen, if one examined his work sufficiently closely, to have been a propagandist for dictatorship, as Hegel and Marx were after him. It was imperative, therefore, to finally critically analyze these great intellectual figures and strip them of the enchantment they had hitherto exercised. This Popper did in his book *The Open Society and Its Enemies*. In the first volume he critiques Plato, and in the second Hegel and Marx, as preparers of the way for totalitarianism. Popper himself says of this book:

> It appeared in 1945, when the war in Europe was already coming to an end, but I had written it as my contribution to the war effort.[43]

What Popper criticizes in Plato is above all this latter's model of an ideal state, which Popper saw as a barely disguised dictatorship. Plato's ideal state is indeed, he insisted, no democracy but rather an "aristocracy" or "government by the best" in the literal sense of the Ancient Greek terms *aristos*, "the best", and *kratos*, "the ruler".

Democracy, in fact, had appeared to Plato to be a very dangerous form of government, since the person whom the mass of the people would elect to be head of the state would, it had seemed to Plato, not necessarily be the best person for this function but rather the one who spoke in the "loudest tones" and made the largest promises. Since the essential thing in Plato's doctrine of Ideas is to develop the soul to ever higher levels and to come to know the Idea of the Good then the state itself, in Plato's view, can be governed only by men who are capable of doing these things. For Plato, philosophers alone can meet such standards, which is why the individuals he proposes as rulers and governors of his ideal state are "philosopher-kings". In Plato's vision, just who among a state's population is suitable for becoming a "philosopher-king" is established via a process requiring tremendous social effort and the individuals, once identified, take up their function only after a lengthy

education and training and the passing of a whole series of tests and examinations. Although, in Plato's
vision, all young male citizens are accorded the right
to take part in these tests, the end result of them is
a society divided into three classes: firstly, the farm-
ers and merchants; then the so-called "guardians"
who, as policemen and soldiers, ensure the peace of
the state; and finally the "philosopher-kings" themselves. Since, however, it is in the end the "philosopher-kings" alone who decide and determine all political affairs within this ideal Platonic state, the only
fair descriptions for this latter are indeed: a dictatorship, and a rigidly divided class society.

Plato, explains Popper, prescribes that the "guardians" and the "philosopher-kings", both of them
highly trained and educated in the specific functions
that they are to fulfil, should live, without any personal property of their own, cut off from the rest of
the population in commune-like compounds. The
"guardians", as we have said, protect the population
from external and internal threats while the "philosopher-kings" take all the essential decisions concern-
ing law and policy. This means, Popper points out,
that the circumstances envisaged for this ideal society closely resemble those applying in and around a
herd of sheep or cattle. The "philosopher-kings" have

the role of the herdsmen; the "guardians" the role of these herdsmen's watch-dogs, keeping the herd in good line and order; and the common folk the role of the passive, obedient herd itself:

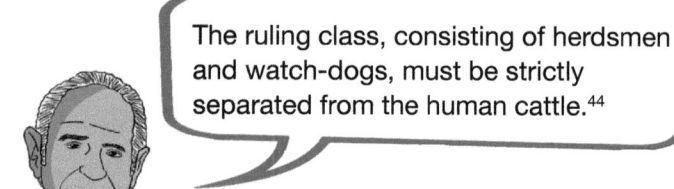

> The ruling class, consisting of herdsmen and watch-dogs, must be strictly separated from the human cattle.[44]

In Plato's ideal state, Popper points out, the mass of the populace neither has any share in determining the broader political life and policy of the state nor do they have any way or opportunity to criticize the "philosopher-kings", who do determine these things. This mass of the populace is powerless in its present state and has no way of acquiring an education that might change that state:

> The ruling class has a monopoly [...] of the right to carry arms and to receive education of any kind.[45]

Popper's account, then, of Plato's ideal state runs, in summary, as follows: this ideal state is a closed society, since the individual citizen has no chance at all to take part, as an individual, in its broader affairs of state and governance and thus to bring him- or herself to full realization. Rather, all individual citizens must subjugate their own wills and judgments to the intuitive vision of the transcendent Ideas which the "philosopher-kings" alone possess and from which they derive the laws that they alone prescribe. But even a "philosopher-king", Popper critically points out here, might at some point become mentally unstable or even outright mentally ill. And even in the best imaginable case, whereby such a king would continue his whole life long to govern optimally in full and perfect accordance with the clearly-perceived "Idea of the Good", there would still arise the problem of his successor:

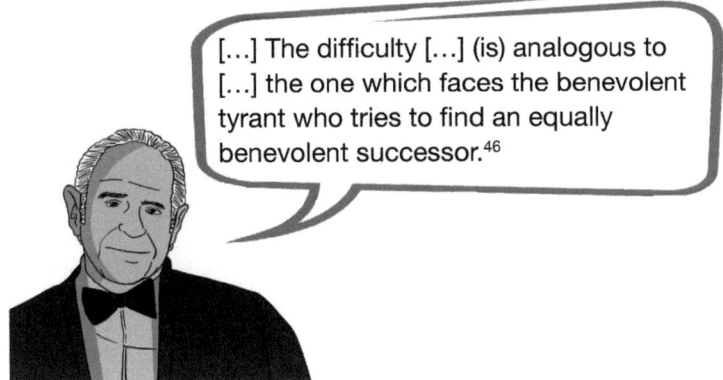

[...] The difficulty [...] (is) analogous to [...] the one which faces the benevolent tyrant who tries to find an equally benevolent successor.[46]

Another serious fault that Popper finds with Plato's ideal state is that he demanded, for anyone contravening the laws of this state, truly Draconian punishments, including solitary confinement and assignment to concentration and re-education camps:

He wanted a dictatorship [...] and in the tenth book of the great work of his old age, *The Laws*, he explains how people of dissenting views must be held in solitary confinement until they recant and, if they never recant, must be punished with death.[47]

Popper refers specifically to the following passage from *The Laws*: "And if anyone be cast (i.e. found guilty), the court shall estimate the punishment of each act of impiety [...] There shall be three prisons in the state. The first of them is to be the common prison in the neighbourhood of the agora [...] Another is to be in the neighbourhood of the nocturnal council and is to be called 'the House of Reformation'. Another, to be situated in some wild and desolate region in the centre of the country, shall be called by some name expressive of retribution [...] Let those who have been made what they are (i.e. lawbreakers) only by want of understanding [...] be placed by the judge in the House of Reformation and ordered to suffer imprisonment during a period of not less than five years. And in the meantime let them have no intercourse with the other citizens except [...] with a view to the improvement of their soul's health. And when the time of their imprisonment is expired, if any of them is of sound mind let him be restored to sane company but if not [...] let him be punished with death."[48]

In addition to this "House of Reformation", however, there is, as we have noted, also another prison or prisons "situated in some wild and desolate region". Popper calls these prisons envisaged by Plato "concentration camps", not least because the prisoners there are stated to be held in solitary confinement. He refers to a passage from the same chapter of *The Laws* in which Plato, after specifying a set of particularly serious deviations from the mores of his ideal state committed by especially "heinous natures", writes: "Let him who is guilty of any of these things be condemned by the court to be bound according to law in the prison which is in the centre of the land,

and let no freeman ever approach him, but let him receive the rations of food appointed (for him) [...] from the hands of the public slaves. And when he is dead let him be cast beyond the borders unburied."[49]

For Popper, then, there can be no doubt but that Plato did indeed demand the establishment of something like "re-education camps" and "concentration camps" Nor can there be any doubt about Plato's utter contempt for the "common people", whom he recommends treating as if they were mere cattle:

One can, of course, explain away much of this by reference to the age that Plato lived in and to his specific situation. But the fact remains that he did have this idea of a 'sub-human' class of human beings. These he felt were to be treated like cattle or sheep.[50]

In Plato's vision of things, it is the "guardians" and the "philosopher-kings" alone that are in possession of the truth. The essence of the open society, by contrast, consists in the fact that every member of such a society is able to bring his or her own truth to the table, regardless of whether they are a leading politician or just an ordinary citizen. Above all, however, it is imperative that, in the open society, each person who raises a claim to truth should be able and willing to practice self-criticism and to concede that they might possibly be in error. It was by envisaging his "philosopher-kings" as infallible that Plato had taken the essential step toward making the ideal state he sketched out a totalitarian one, with no room for either critique or falsification. Furthermore, the question that Plato had posed in his political philosophy had been, from the very beginning, the wrong question:

Plato formulated the problem in the following way: *Who should rule? The few or the many?* His answer was: The best should rule! That would also have been the answer given by Mussolini or by Hitler. [51]

Not only Plato's answer, then, but also his central question had been erroneous. Rather than the question "*who* should rule?" the question that ought to have been asked was: "*how* should rulership be exercised?" For Popper, the most decisive consideration for anyone attempting to work out a theory or philosophy of government must be:

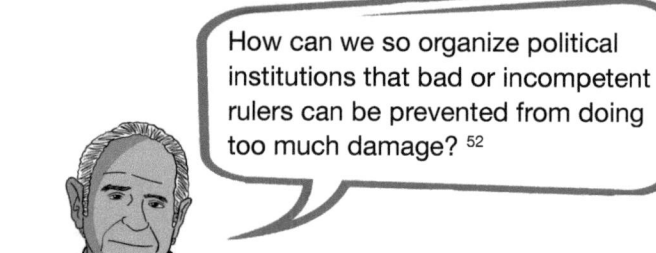

> How can we so organize political institutions that bad or incompetent rulers can be prevented from doing too much damage? [52]

Popper's own answer to this question is: by limiting the period for which any particular government can rule, so that, if the worst occurs, a bad government can, as in the natural-scientific procedure of "trial and error", be recognized as an "error", which can then be "corrected" by being replaced:

> The most important aspect of democracy is that it provides the possibility of deposing a government without shots having to be fired. [53]

In Popper's view, democracy is the form of state and government which needs logically to be adopted by any society aspiring to be an open society. When there were pointed out to him the many problems that come with democracy, such as the fact that under this system it is often not the citizens but rather parties and lobbyists for large economic interests that end up ruling, Popper would often cite Winston Churchill:

Churchill, who was a good democrat, once said: 'Democracy is the worst form of government – except for all those other forms that have been tried from time to time'.[54]

Democracy makes control by elections possible. But the "philosopher-kings" in Plato's ideal state can never be controlled, voted out, or deposed. It is for this reason that we may speak of Plato as the first representative of totalitarianism. His fateful legacy was taken up, in the modern era, by Hegel and Marx.

The False Prophets Hegel and Marx

Popper sees Hegel and Marx too as thinkers who prepared the way for twentieth-century totalitarianism. He develops his reasons for seeing them in this way in the second large volume of his book *The Open Society and Its Enemies*, which he entitled *The High Tide of Prophecy: Hegel, Marx and the Aftermath*. In this second volume of his political-philosophical masterpiece Popper portrays these two great 19th-century German thinkers as prophets indeed, but decidedly false prophets. The "prophecies" made by these thinkers, in the form of their claims and prognoses regarding the necessary course of history, were, Popper argues, both obscure and completely unreliable. They claimed to have grasped and understood human history's dialectical law of motion. And not only this: Hegel and Marx even claimed to have identified what the ultimate "goal" and "end" of human history had necessarily to be. This, from the point of view of the constantly questioning and "falsifying" open society that Popper wished to defend, was a finalistic determinism that could not be permitted to stand.

Hegel, indeed, had even contended that the "goal of history" had already, in his own lifetime, been achieved. He argued that at the end and high-point of the long process of "the self-unfolding of the World-Spirit" that had carried Man from barbarism to civilization there stood that very Prussian constitutional monarchy of which he was himself a citizen:

Hegel's philosophy was a deification of the state, and specifically of the Prussian state. He even declared this Prussian state to embody 'the march of God through the world'.[55]

It should, admittedly, be granted to Hegel that the state that he so glorifies in his philosophy of history is indeed the constitutionally-structured state of the modern era, which he looks on as a great step forward vis-à-vis the forms of state and government that had predominated in the Middle Ages and in the ancient world. Modern constitutional states, Hegel had pointed out, had, with their constitutions and codes of civil law, provided their citizens, for the first time in history, with a certain legal security and had also seen to it that all were absolutely equal before the laws in question. Popper concurred with Hegel, of course, in looking on the introduction of constitutions into state organization as a hugely important progress. But he was strongly critical of that aspect of Hegel's philosophy that glorified the constitutional state above all as a state and that tended to rank the state in all its forms above the individual, to the point of stripping this latter of all his or her rights:

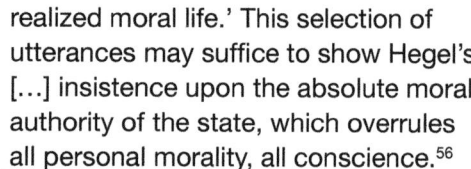

(For Hegel) the state is everything and the individual nothing [...] 'The Universal is to be found in the State', Hegel writes. 'The State is the Divine Idea as it exists on earth [...] The State is the actually existing,

realized moral life.' This selection of utterances may suffice to show Hegel's [...] insistence upon the absolute moral authority of the state, which overrules all personal morality, all conscience.[56]

Besides this excessive glorification of the state as the sole source of all ethics, morality and law Hegel also committed, Popper argues, a second, equally consequential error. Hegel had recognized that there existed between the states of the modern world no power or law outside of and above these states, no "praetor" to use Hegel's own term, that might settle, as a neutral party, disputes between them. It was for this reason that wars between states sometimes occurred. Popper cites, and comments on, the following passage from Hegel:

'The relations of state to state are uncertain and there is no praetor there to adjust them' […] Hegel can therefore identify '[…] the true result of the

world's history': to be successful; that is, to emerge as the strongest from the dialectical struggle of the different National Spirits for power, for world domination […].[57]

With his description of the state as the foreordained realization on earth of the World Spirit, combined with this description of a possible struggle between several states for global dominance, Hegel, argued Popper, had laid the foundation for the later totalitarian worldviews of both Marx and Hitler. Because, Popper contends:

> Marx replaced Hegel's 'Spirit' [...] by material and economic interests. In the same way, racialism substitutes for Hegel's 'Spirit' the quasi-biological conception of Blood or Race. Instead of 'Spirit' [...] Blood is now the sovereign of the world and displays itself on the Stage of History.[58]

Marx, points out Popper, simply puts "class struggle" in place of "the self-unfolding of the World Spirit". In Marx's vision, consequently, human historical development in its entirety is just a long series of class struggles which give rise, one after the other, to new forms of society, from slave society through feudal society right down to our own society dominated, according to Marx, by the "bourgeoisie". But even in this bourgeoisie-dominated society, argues Marx, those working-class citizens whom the bourgeoisie dominates and exploits are becoming ever more numerous and more important for the productive process. And since the pressure placed on the bourgeois capitalists to "rationalize" their enterprises is tending to drive more and more members of this huge class of people into utter poverty, there must inevitably eventually result a workers' revolution, followed by the establishment of socialism and of a classless society. But in making this "prophecy", argues Popper, Marx proved himself a "false prophet":

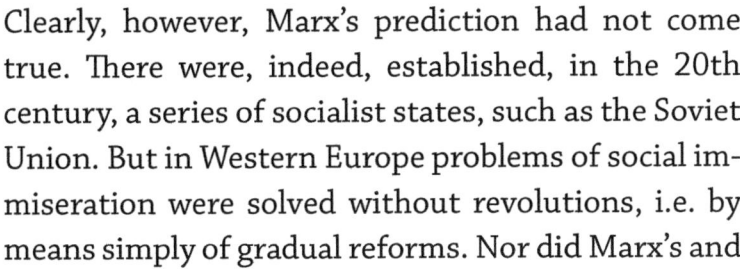

It was Marx's attempt to prove by historical science that a socialist revolution had to come about sooner or later [...] The advent of socialism was, according to Marx, something that could be infallibly predicted if one only applied his 'scientific' theory of history, just as one can predict a solar eclipse by applying astronomical science.[59]

Clearly, however, Marx's prediction had not come true. There were, indeed, established, in the 20th century, a series of socialist states, such as the Soviet Union. But in Western Europe problems of social immiseration were solved without revolutions, i.e. by means simply of gradual reforms. Nor did Marx's and

Engels's prediction of a "dictatorship of the proletariat" ever come true in the form that Marx and Engels had envisaged:

> The Russian revolution showed that – quite contrary to what Marx had believed – socialism was in no sense a 'dictatorship of the proletariat' but rather the dictatorship of a party, which soon itself became a new ruling class [...].[60]

It was not, however, Popper argued, these particular errors of Marx's that made his philosophy of history such a dangerous one but rather his most basic and general prediction to the effect that human history had a specific and predetermined "goal" or "meaning":

> The revolution is coming: this Marx believed he had proven. It followed, then, that we must help it on its way.[61]

A belief like this led inevitably, Popper points out, to anyone who did not wish to join in the revolution and the implementation of socialism, and most certainly anyone who had the temerity to propose some alternative course to this, being branded a "class enemy" and accused of standing in the way of historical progress. In the very last chapter of his *Open Society and Its Enemies* Popper poses this key question: "has history any meaning?" His answer leaves his readers in no doubt:

> *History has no meaning* [...]
> This must be the reply of every humanitarian.[62]

All those who claim, then, that they understand the meaning or goal of history are, Popper contends, "false prophets" and will tend to bring disaster upon Mankind if they are believed. Marx, with his theory of the dictatorship of the proletariat, had provided the foundation for the decades-long oppression of the population of the so-called "socialist countries". Hitler, with his philosophy of history envisaging a struggle between races and a predestined victory and domination of the Aryan race, had led the whole world into a terrible war. Popper, therefore, in another key political-philosophical book, *The Poverty of Historicism*, critiques all such prophets and their prophecies as pernicious for mankind, since they tend to prevent the development of the open society:

If we wish to avoid tipping the world once again into catastrophe we need to give up on our dreams of bringing total happiness to the entire world [...] We need rather to content ourselves with the never-

ending task of easing human suffering and battling against those evils which we know can be prevented.[63]

This must occur via a large number of small reforms, i.e. according to the principle of "trial and error". Thus, we learn from our mistakes and thereby improve the world. Those thinkers, however, who believe that history as a whole has become transparent to them and that they can predict its necessary end and meaning Popper calls "historicists":

The idea that one can make historical predictions of this sort is [...] historicism.[64]

Both Hegel and Marx had been "historicists" in this sense.

Popper mounted this critique of historicism at a point in time at which a whole third of humanity were living in societies whose governments explicitly declared their allegiance to Marx and to Marxism. But even today, after the fall of the Iron Curtain and the self-dissolution of the socialist states of Eastern Europe, Popper's warning against ideologies that claim to be able to prescribe an aim for history still applies:

[...] If there is such a thing as growing human knowledge, then we cannot anticipate today what we shall know only tomorrow.[65]

Critical Rationalism as Constant Renewal of Knowledge and Society

Instead of the gigantic social utopia of a classless society we need, argues Popper, the constant improvement of the conditions of our lives by means of rational self-criticism and reforms. This was the reason why Popper founded his own style and school of philosophy, which went by the name: "Critical Rationalism".

In the end, Popper insists, the same principle applies both to politics and to the hard sciences. The only knowledge we can possibly have is conjectural knowledge. Consequently, we are obliged to constantly undertake the falsification of our theories, using the procedure of trial and error, and, where these prove indeed to be false, to give them up in favour of others:

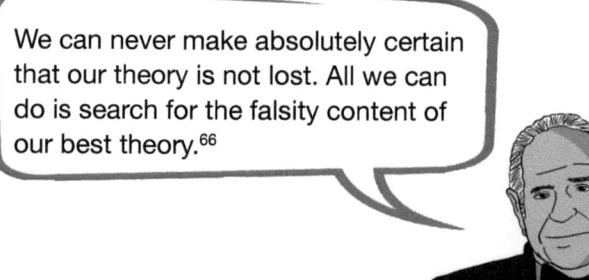

We can never make absolutely certain that our theory is not lost. All we can do is search for the falsity content of our best theory.[66]

This applies also, and indeed quite especially, to the social sciences and to politics. Each reform, each general social project and each plan for the improvement of society might potentially be an error. This is something that all the world's politicians must be kept keenly aware of:

> Every person who involves themselves in politics in any way [...] must be mindful of the fact that they know nothing and must be prepared to learn

> [...] They must constantly critique themselves and constantly be trying to improve their own theories regarding state and society.[67]

It is to just this self-critical attitude of mind that Popper gives the name "Critical Rationalism":

> (The Critical Rationalism that I defend) is an attitude of readiness to listen to critical arguments and to learn from experience.[68]

Both scientists and politicians, then, must remain modest, humble and capable of engaging in dialogue and accepting criticism. They should take to heart that famous saying of Socrates: "I know only that I know nothing."

A key figure of reference, indeed, for Popper's "Critical Rationalism" is Socrates as he is portrayed in the earliest-written of Plato's "Socratic dialogues", such as *The Apology*. It is such early works of Plato's, Popper contends, and these alone, that provide a true and correct portrait of the real historical Socrates and of his real attitude of mind. And if this Socrates of the early dialogues is indeed the true Socrates, then Socrates, Popper further concludes, was a "falsificationist" just like himself. The famous saying just cited, in which Socrates declares that he "knows only that he knows nothing" means, on Popper's interpretation of it, that for Socrates as for Popper himself there is no timeless truth by which we are eternally bound and that the very best we can do is attempt conjectural approaches to truth. Plato, Popper argues, had given a faithful portrait of this "falsificationist" Socrates in such early dialogues as *The Apology*. But in his later dialogues he had retained the character of Socrates and misleadingly presented him as a proponent of Plato's own decidedly non-

and anti-"falsificationist" doctrine of eternal Ideas. Since Socrates left no writings of his own and almost all that we believe we know of him does indeed stem from the dialogues composed by his student Plato, it is difficult, or even impossible, to judge how true this accusation that Plato misused and misrepresented his teacher might be. Popper, in any case, opts to cite in support of his own position a Socrates who was in no way a proponent of timelessly valid, transcendent "Ideas". The sense in which Popper, and the Socrates he cites as his precursor, understands "ideas" is one which demands a constant checking, over time, of these latter's truth:

Our ideas can, if we are sufficiently open to it, be constantly corrected by reality.[69]

Since this applies equally both to the natural sciences and to such social sciences as politics, there will be needed in future an entirely new form and way of governing political states. Popper recommends the introduction of something called "social technology". That is to say, politicians must, in essence, become "social engineers" or rather, as Popper is careful to specify, practitioners of "piecemeal social engineering". Such politicians would proceed exactly as practitioners of the "hard sciences" should do, i.e. they would first work out hypotheses regarding ways in which social conditions could be improved; they would then apply these hypotheses in a closely controlled and monitored way; in this way, they would be able to establish, by a process of trial and error, which of these should be discontinued as provenly erroneous and which should be persisted in:

The characteristic approach of the piecemeal engineer is this. Even though he may perhaps cherish some ideals that concern society 'as a whole' – its general welfare, perhaps – he does not believe in the method of redesigning it as a whole. Whatever his ends, he tries to achieve them by small adjustments and re-adjustments which can be continually improved upon.[70]

Of What Use is Popper's Discovery for Us Today?

Popper's Notion of the "Step-by-Step Improvement of Life"

Of what use to us is Popper's discovery in the end? His "Critical Rationalism" gained, early on, much support among practicing scientists. Above all certain well-known physicists, such as Einstein, welcomed Popper's new approach. But if one follows later developments right up to our own present day, one cannot help but recognize that "Critical Rationalism" has gained only limited long-term acceptance both as regards the theory and as regards the actual practice of the natural sciences. Falsification, indeed, has come to be recognized as an essential element in the critique of any theory. In practice, however, it continues to be predominantly inductive and empirical procedures that are followed and respected in the process of legitimation of such theories. The principle is still widely accepted: the larger the number of case studies and empirical findings that seem to go to verify a theory, the more believable is its claim to truth.

Politicians, on the other hand, have taken up "Critical Rationalism" with great interest and enthusiasm. Today, politicians of almost every party declare themselves to be committed to promoting and maintaining "the open society". After the experiences of Fascism, National Socialism and Stalinism Popper's key idea of a tolerant political culture capable of practicing self-criticism at any time has become a basic pillar of modern democracies. Popper's argument that it is impossible to free the world, at a single stroke, from all suffering has also become an almost universally shared opinion:

There can be no perfect society.[71]

The former German Chancellor Helmut Schmidt, for example, publicly declared the central importance of Popper's work for his own idea of how politics and statecraft should be conducted. He made the following recommendation to his fellow Social Democrats: "Every Social Democrat should read Marx. But they should also read Popper." [72] Social Democrats, Schmidt argued, should give up, once and for all, the utopian idea of a revolutionary restructuring of society in favour of a reform-oriented social policy. The old ideal of socialism had to be replaced, as a vision of the way forward, by that of a step-by-step improvement of social conditions, carried out in the modest, self-critical way that Popper had proposed:

Try looking at the world as a beautiful open square which we can cultivate and improve as if it were a garden. And try applying, as you imagine this, the modesty and humility of an experienced gardener, who knows that many of his attempts at beautification will not succeed. [73]

But an equally well-respected German Chancellor of the opposite party, Helmut Kohl of the Christian Democrats, also declared Popper's ideas to form an important part of his personal political philosophy, seeing in Popper a precursor of his own conservatism. Both Schmidt and Kohl must have been all the more disappointed, then, as it became clearer and clearer that Popper aligned himself, in politics, with the "liberal" current. He had, indeed, already in 1947 been one of the founders, along with Friedrich von Hayek and Milton Friedman, of the "Mont Pelerin Society", an associated intended to propagate worldwide the basic ideas of economic liberalism. Popper himself liked to call himself "the liberal with the razor", since he also, despite his economic liberalism, strongly criticized the excesses of the capitalist economic model.

But his political legacy consists, in the last analysis, above all in his call to contemporary mankind to resist the temptations of all totalitarian ideologies, forgo all attempts to overthrow existing society by revolution, and concentrate on improving the world in small steps.

Is Popper Right? Did Plato, Hegel and Marx Prepare the Way for Totalitarianism?

> Already before 1848 the Germans were faced with a decision: Kant or Hegel? Were they to choose peace or the power of the state? To their great misfortune they chose Hegel [...].[74]

In the first place here one must oppose to this claim of Popper's the simple objection that he surely greatly overestimates the influence exerted by Kant and Hegel. Far more than 90 per cent of Germans have never read Kant, let alone understood him. And one can be sure that the number of those who have read and understood Hegel is many times smaller still. Even Goethe ended up despairing of ever understanding those works of Hegel's that he read and had to personally request of the latter philosopher that he explain the dialectic to him as he would to a child. Hegel's response was that all he needed to do in order to grasp the dialectic was to recall the "spirit of gain-saying" that had been in Goethe as a child, as it is in all children. Dialectic, explained Hegel, was nothing other than the ordered, methodically developed form of this child-like impulse to contradict everything, which persists beyond childhood in every human be-ing and which is an important motor of the progress of science and knowledge. It may be that Goethe un-derstood Hegel better after this explanation; but it is certain that very few of his German contemporaries enjoyed the same eventual success in understanding this deeply obscure philosopher. Popper, nonethe-less, insisted that German intellectuals, quite espe-cially, remained for many decades profoundly under the influence of the philosophical education that Hegel had imparted to the thinkers, poets and other cultured men of the early 19th century:

I believe that the First World War would never have been able to break out if German intellectuals had not been mentally paralyzed by this education.[75]

There can be little doubt but that, with historically sweeping statements like this, Popper accords rather too much weight to the influence of Hegel's philosophical theory of the state. And his drastic judgment of Plato, Hegel and Marx as "thinkers who prepared the way for totalitarianism" has indeed, quite generally, been subjected to severe criticism by other scholars and philosophers.

With regard to Plato, for example, the question has been raised against Popper of whether it is really possible to describe as "totalitarian" an ideal state like Plato's, which is stated to be ruled by well-trained and -educated "philosopher-kings" who will have undergone repeated tests of whether their characters are apt for such a function. These Platonic "philosopher-kings", so Popper's critics have objected, have a sworn duty to promote the education of the soul to higher and higher tasks in the service of the Idea of the Good, the True and the Beautiful, so that their pursuing political courses and measures displaying a contempt for human beings is simply out of the question.

Popper and his students, however, have generally remained unconvinced by these objections. Whether or not the actions of the "philosopher-kings" actually do bring to realization the "Idea of the Good" is,

Popper and the Popperians counter-object, impossible to verify or establish, since Plato nowhere gives a really concrete account of just what he means by "the Good". The rule of the "philosopher-kings", then, is one that can never be subjected to any rational criticism or critique. And it is just for this reason that it is a totalitarian rule.

In the case of Popper's critique of Hegel, what Popper focuses on is above all Hegel's impenetrably obscure mode of expression:

I consider Hegel, and to an even greater extent Heidegger, to be philosophically utterly empty and uninteresting chauvinists.[76]

One cannot prove to them that what they are saying is false for the simple reason that it is incomprehensible [...].[77]

Popper's criticism, then, is that it is impossible to "falsify" Hegel's philosophy, i.e. prove it to be erroneous, because the claims that he makes in it cannot be understood in the first place:

I contend that one encounters, again and again, passages in Hegel that are expressed in such vague and difficult terms that it is impossible to know just what he is really trying to say, or

indeed if he is trying to say anything [...] One can't stop him and say 'My dear Hegel, that is wrong.' Because it

isn't clear what it is, it also can't be clear that it's wrong.[78]

It speaks in Popper's favour that he openly admits to not having fully understood Hegel. And in fact scholarship does tend, today, to take it as beyond dispute that Popper's interpretation especially of Hegel's philosophy of "Spirit" was one that displayed huge gaps in comprehension.[79]

This is certainly a pity, since Hegel's philosophy of the gradual evolution of the "World Spirit" displays, in fact, a certain affinity to Popper's own theory of knowledge. Because Hegel too proceeds, just as Popper does, on the assumption that, initially at least, there exists no absolute truth but rather only a permanent gradual movement of approach to this latter. Thus, for Hegel as for Popper, each epoch of science creates its own truth: a truth which bears up and subsists only up to the point where it is refuted and dialectically relieved by a new and better truth or, as both Hegel and Popper phrase it, "raised up to a higher level". We find in Hegel passages which describe that which had previously been taken to be true "becoming a simple shading of itself" [80] in a manner remarkably anticipative of Popper's theory of science, whereby each new theory relieves the one previously accepted as soon as this latter has been falsified.

Just this is the meaning of what is perhaps Hegel's most famous dictum: "The true is the whole; however, the whole is only the essence completing itself through its own development". [81] Whether and when the development toward the complete truth will be concluded are questions that Hegel leaves as open as Popper himself does. It is indeed clearly stated in

Hegel's philosophy that the dialectical truth-process must culminate, at some point, in "absolute knowledge", i.e. in a state of perfect concordance between knowledge and reality. But Popper too implicitly presupposes this same final goal of the knowledge-process in the form of an absolute concordance of theory and reality. He conceded as much in an interview with the French magazine *L'Express*:

> It is only by reference to some absolute truth that we can become aware of how little we know [...] But this notion of absolute truth is also important for another reason [...] It is a bulwark against relativism which is only too comfortable with the notion that truth does not exist.[82]

In the last analysis, then, Popper defended, just like Hegel, the supposition of an absolute truth. Popper's accusation against Hegel that he had illegitimately cut short this absolute truth, and the end of the evolving dialectical process, by seeing them both as coming to completion already in the Prussian constitutional monarchy and in a struggle between states for world domination is not, in fact, an accusation that finds support in Hegel's text.

What is more, despite his glorification of the Prussian state which Popper rightly criticizes, Hegel was by no means a nationalist but rather a convinced supporter and defender of human rights and the values of the Enlightenment just like Popper himself. He writes in his *Philosophy of Right* that "*a human being counts as such because he is a human being*, not because he is a Jew, Catholic, Protestant, German, Italian etc." [83] Furthermore, Hegel views, just as Popper does, human historical development as "the progress of consciousness toward freedom" and even lays special emphasis on the increase over time of individualism, equality before the law and civic freedom.

In short, then: the similarities between the two thinkers are so striking that one might describe Popper as, in many respects, a modern Hegelian, even if he would turn in his grave at being characterized in this way.

The one true difference between the two thinkers consists in the fact that, in Hegel's work, the whole development of life and science from its simplest beginnings right up to today takes the form of a threefold dialectical self-development: firstly, the unfolding of human consciousness; secondly, the unfolding of world history; and thirdly, the unfolding of the metaphysical "World Spirit", although all these movements are, in the end, just different perspectives on one and the same process of dialectical "self-sublation". In Popper's thought too, indeed, the unfolding of life and science is a kind of "self-moving motion", although in this case it must be specified that it is, at least initially, a purely biological "self-motion", driven forward by mutation and natural selection:

From the very beginning, most probably through some Darwinian process of natural selection, life seeks a better world.[84]

It is only later that human consciousness becomes a factor in this process and begins to play its part in furthering the development:

All organisms are constantly posing and solving problems; consequently, science is really nothing else but a continuation of an activity already carried out by the lower organisms.[85]

When it comes right down to it, then, Popper and Hegel display more similarities to, than differences from, one another in their ways of thinking. For this reason, we may be sure that Hegel was not really, as Popper claims, a "pre-totalitarian". Like his critique of Hegel, Popper's critique of Marx has earned sharp contradiction from many scholars. There is surely no doubting the fact that Marx himself was a humanist and attempted to make the world a better place. Popper himself, indeed, concedes as much:

Marx showed that he lived in a world in which, on the one hand, there was oppression and exploitation and, on the other, luxury. In this regard, his work is certainly of great merit.[86]

But despite this appreciation of Marx's merits Popper stuck by the fundamental substance of his critique of this philosopher:

In spite of his merits Marx was, I believe, a false prophet.[87]

Just like Plato with his ideal state Marx had attempted, with his vision of the setting-up of a classless society, to establish a kind of heaven on earth. But in attempting such a thing, argues Popper, Marx had undertaken a project which was mistaken in its very essence and foredoomed to fail:

[...] The attempt to make heaven on earth invariably produces hell. It leads to intolerance. It leads to religious wars and to the saving of souls through the Inquisition.[88]

Whether Marx can, as Popper claims, be made responsible, by reason of his historical determinism, for the dictatorial structures that existed in the countries of "really existing socialism" is a matter of speculation and thus a question that cannot be answered.

Any fair and balanced judgment, then, on Popper's more-than-thousand-page-long political-philosophical masterpiece *The Open Society and Its Enemies* would have to recognize that, while Popper on the one hand surely "overshot the mark" in some respects in his critique of Plato, Hegel and Marx as the main pavers of the way for dictatorship, racism and totalitarianism, his aggressive and disrespectful manner of dealing with these great thinkers also, on the other, made an important contribution to modern intellectual culture. What Popper is concerned with, at bottom, is the unmasking of long-revered philosophical monuments from a completely new perspective: namely, that of Critical Rationalism and the open society. With his attack on these three eminent thinkers Popper is setting for us, his readers, the example of a certain intellectual attitude. He wants to encourage us to apply uncompromisingly to all individuals and epochs of history this standard of the open society and of democracy, so as to school and train in all areas our critical self-awareness. Popper believed that this new perspective of Critical Rationalism needed to be applied not only to such revered intellectual titans as Plato, Hegel and Marx but also to such historical figures as Julius Caesar:

We are no longer prepared to accord to the great criminals of history the adoration that they were long accorded. Not to Julius Caesar, for example,

who laid France to waste, stuck all the booty from this destruction into his own pocket and returned to Rome as the richest man in the world.[89]

And indeed one might well pose, with Popper, this question of whether the teaching of history in our schools is not in need of a fundamental and thoroughgoing reform. It is not just the positive image that is taught to us of Caesar, who did indeed replace the quasi-democratic structures of ancient Rome with a dictatorship, that is problematical. Our history books still speak of "Alexander the Great".

But from the viewpoint of democratic theory, i.e. from the viewpoint of Critical Rationalism, Alexander was anything but a "great" figure. Considered from this latter perspective, he was simply someone who subjugated, with the aid of ten thousand mercenaries, an entire continent, levelled to the ground that great palace at Persepolis that it had taken decades to build, had himself worshipped as a god, and ended up finally murdering or having executed, either in a personal passion or by cold political calculation, all who opposed him. His highly artificial empire, which was held together by violence alone, fell apart just a few years after his death.

To sum up, then: even if Popper sometimes developed his critiques of Plato, of Marx and quite especially of Hegel in an overly aggressive manner, the core idea behind these critiques remains sound and beyond dispute. This core idea is the demand for an open society and an urging of us never again to yield to the temptation of giving credence to historicistic prognoses positing a supposed "end and goal of history":

The future depends on ourselves, and we do not depend on any historical necessity.[90]

The Positivism Dispute: Critical Rationalism Instead of Critical Theory?

His whole life long Popper remained an extremely disputatious thinker. Equipped with his new method of Critical Rationalism he never shied away from any fight. It was inevitable, then, that in 1961 he became involved in a second great polemical engagement, this time not with the great, long-dead intellectual eminences Hegel and Marx themselves but with two of his own contemporaries, Adorno and Habermas, who, as the most important living members of the so-called "Frankfurt School", represented the 20th-century continuation and development of the Hegelian and Marxist philosophical traditions. This polemical engagement has gone down in intellectual history as "the positivism dispute in German sociology" and is still often discussed even today.

Popper developed his central idea in two phases. In the first phase he published, primarily in the form of his book *The Logic of Scientific Discovery*, his new theory of knowledge, whereby every scientific theory consists only of conjectural knowledge and can be allowed, therefore, to persist only up to the point where it is falsified. In the second phase, beginning with his book *The Open Society and Its Enemies*, he transposed this originally natural-science-based theory of knowledge into the sphere of the social sciences and of politics. Also psychologists, sociologists and philosophers, Popper now argued, should henceforth propose only theories which are such as to be susceptible of being checked, and potentially falsified, by the method of "trial and error".

The first time that Popper raised this demand on the social sciences in full and systematic form was at the 1961 Tübingen conference of the German Society of Sociology. The renowned sociologist Ralf Dahrendorf had invited some of Germany's most eminent social theorists to debate with one another there and among these eminent thinkers were Popper and the Critical Theorist Adorno. It was Popper who delivered the main opening address to the conference's plenary session, dealing at length with the controversial topic of *The Logic of the Social Sciences*. In twenty-seven theses Popper expounded to his audience of social scientists the manner of proceeding which he viewed to be the imperative, because only scientifically correct one for their disciplines. His address provoked passionate resistance and contradiction. Primarily due to the fact that in the sixth of these theses, which was to become perhaps the most famous or notorious of the twenty-seven, Popper urged the assembled social scientists to advance, much after the manner of practitioners of the "hard" sciences, henceforth no longer general but only individual hypotheses, which could then either be empirically supported by certain observable events, facts and measurements or, in the case where the facts and events failed to support them, be criticized and rejected as false:

> The method of the social sciences, like that of the natural sciences, consists in trying out tentative solutions [...] Solutions are proposed and criticized.[91]

And this means that:

If a proposed solution is not open to pertinent criticism, then it is excluded as non-scientific [...].[92]

At first sight, views like these may appear moderate and almost harmless. In the context of the German sociologists' debates of the early 1960s, however, accepting these views would have had grave consequences for many. If, as Popper demands here, all "tentative solutions" and theories which are not accessible to critical checking and examination in the form of falsification really are to be "excluded as non-scientific", then the social theory of the Frankfurt School, for example, is rendered "non-scientific", that is to say intellectually impermissible, at a single stroke. And indeed, Popper came straight out and accused the sociological approach adopted by Adorno of being a form of "obscurantism".[93]

Adorno, for example, argued Popper, took as his point of departure for his famously anti-capitalist sociology, the assumption of the alienation and falsity of the whole capitalist system. It was from this all-embracing standpoint, summed up in his famous dictum "the whole is the false", that he developed his critiques of individual events and processes. This claim, however, that the capitalist mode of production and consumption is "false" as a whole, in each and every aspect, is a claim that can be neither falsified nor refuted. So that, the theory of Adorno and of the entire Frankfurt School being unfalsifiable, it was also, on Popper's definition, "unscientific".

Adorno and Habermas, on their side, criticized Popper's approach, based on the methods of the natural sciences, as naïve. Popper and other people trained in the "hard sciences", they claimed, tended to lack all capacity to reflect upon their own limited ways of seeing and approaching sociological problems. "Hard scientists", argued Adorno, never allow anything to count as "true" except that which they are unable to falsify or refute. Conversely, they hold everything to be true that presents itself to them as a positive fact, i.e. that they can measure and recreate under experimental conditions. They thereby lose sight, however, of every truth that may be of more complex nature than this and not directly measurable. Moreover, they cannot allow themselves to admit either to themselves or to others that the so-called "scientific studies" that they produce are in fact always carried out from specific, far from neutral perspectives imposed on them by the power calculations of governments or the corporate goals and capital interests of commissioning private enterprises. Only a theory like his own "Critical Theory", argued Adorno in retort to Popper's polemical "sixth thesis", was equipped to identify and understand, thanks to its justified suspicion of the capitalist system "as a whole", these multifarious interests behind all supposedly objective science.

It made, then, no sense at all, Adorno went on to specify, for sociologists to do as Popper asked and focus their researches on isolated, individual themes and problems, such as family, authorities, peer groups or mass media, and to advance hypotheses relating to these individual spheres alone without at the same time critiquing the general form of society which, by using these as its "psycho-social agencies", alone makes them what they in practice actually are. If Popper, argued Adorno, were to be allowed to compel, as he aspired to do, all sociologists to limit their work to falsifiable individual aspects of society, the result would be that all true sociological knowledge would become impossible. Only a critical theory of society, equipped with an idea of the whole and a vision of an intact and undamaged human intersubjectivity, could possibly hope to fulfil the task of a critical sociology. Thus Adorno arrives at the conclusion: "If its concepts are to be true, critical sociology is, according to its own idea, necessarily also a critique of society." [94] Popper's notion, on the other hand, Adorno added, of sociologists' pursuing purely scientific, always empirically verifiable, value-neutral researches was nothing but an illusion, because knowledge and interest are, in capitalist society, inextricably interwoven with one another.

Popper, nonetheless, holds stubbornly to this notion. He views Adorno's generalizing critique of the "whole system" of capitalist society as a merely polemical, fundamentally un-scientific undertaking. One must at all costs, he argues, hold fast to the ideal of objective knowledge and of empirical testability:

It must be possible for an empirical-scientific system to be refuted by experience. [95]

Even if Popper insists that every theory must be bound back and linked to experience, he nonetheless energetically repudiates the accusation that he is a shallow and unreflecting Positivist, who admits the validity of nothing except "positively" perceptible facts:

Whereas Positivism teaches the doctrine 'Stick to what can be perceived', what I have taught has been: 'Be bold in your advancing of speculative hypotheses but once you have advanced them, test and criticize them mercilessly!' [96]

And indeed Popper was not a Positivist, inasmuch as he defended the principle of an absolute freedom to form theories, far beyond the limits set by perception and perceptibility. That the dispute of 1961 about the correct method for sociology has gone down in history as "the Positivism Dispute" is largely due to Habermas, who chose to publish the various contributions to this debate under this latter title. Popper's concern was really, rather than to defend

"Positivism", to motivate scholars in the social sciences to formulate their theories in such a way that they remained, in any case, criticisable:

The objectivity of scientific statements lies in the fact that they can be intersubjectively tested.[97]

Popper's Legacy: All Life is Problem-Solving

Even in the year of his death, 1994, the 92-year-old Popper was still working on one final book. We can look on the title of this book as his legacy and his message to posterity:

All life is problem-solving.[98]

This applies to our personal lives, to science, and above all to politics:

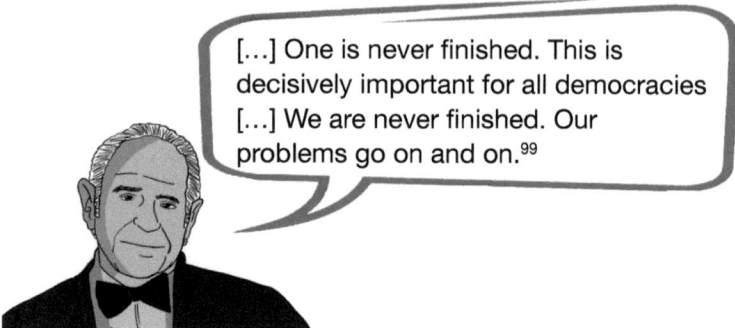

[...] One is never finished. This is decisively important for all democracies [...] We are never finished. Our problems go on and on.[99]

When asked about the most urgent and important problems of our present day, Popper mentioned the explosive growth in world population and also global warming:

The population explosion lies at the root of today's environmental catastrophes [...].[100]

Every additional billion human beings means a massive new sealing of the earth's surface by a thousand new metropolises, whose consumption of land can be seen even from space. Just since 1970 the global population has grown from around 3.6 to over 7 billion people. This spreading of the human species all over the earth is leading to the dying out of many other species, the overheating of agricultural and industrial production, and the loss of the planet's oxygen base. Programmes of contraception, intensive education, and campaigns of global information must be used, argues Popper, to finally put a stop to these fatal trends. As a provisional solution, he adds, it might be possible to reduce CO_2 emissions by biological measures, specifically by making use of those marine sections of the world's surface that have not fallen victim to massive human settling:

We know that all plants live on light and CO_2. One might try, then, to cover the marine surfaces of the planet more thickly with algae than they have been up until now.[101]

These problems of population increase and global warming have become still more serious in the years since Popper expressed these views. But, Popper insists, we must not become overly pessimistic. Mankind has always faced great problems. It would be wrong to discourage younger people from trying to radically improve the world:

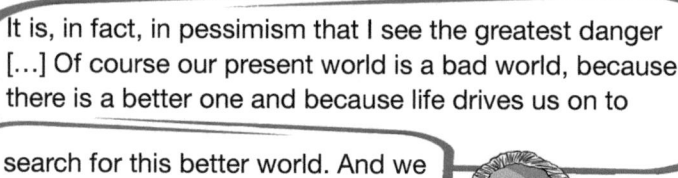

It is, in fact, in pessimism that I see the greatest danger [...] Of course our present world is a bad world, because there is a better one and because life drives us on to search for this better world. And we need to persist in this search.[102]

A broad and embracing view of human evolution, Popper adds, also speaks against any excessively pessimistic view of our situation. Life itself has a tendency never to give up. It tries always to carry on, to find solutions and to raise itself up to higher levels. Popper, indeed, sees the whole course of evolution as, in the last analysis, a great, in fact universal process of problem-solving:

Evolution too proceeds by trial and error. We might look on mutations as 'trials' in this sense [...]. [103]

For example, in order to solve the particular problems of a changing environment, both plants and animals have, since time immemorial, brought forth mutations, so as to fit better into the environments which were transforming around them. In the case where these mutations proved inappropriate to the new surroundings and thus instances of "error" in the "trial and error" process, they were "falsified" and vanished from the earth; in the case, however, where they were successful, they continued to develop and assert themselves right up to the present day. In the last analysis, evolution means one long, bold experimentation with new forms and self-differentiations:

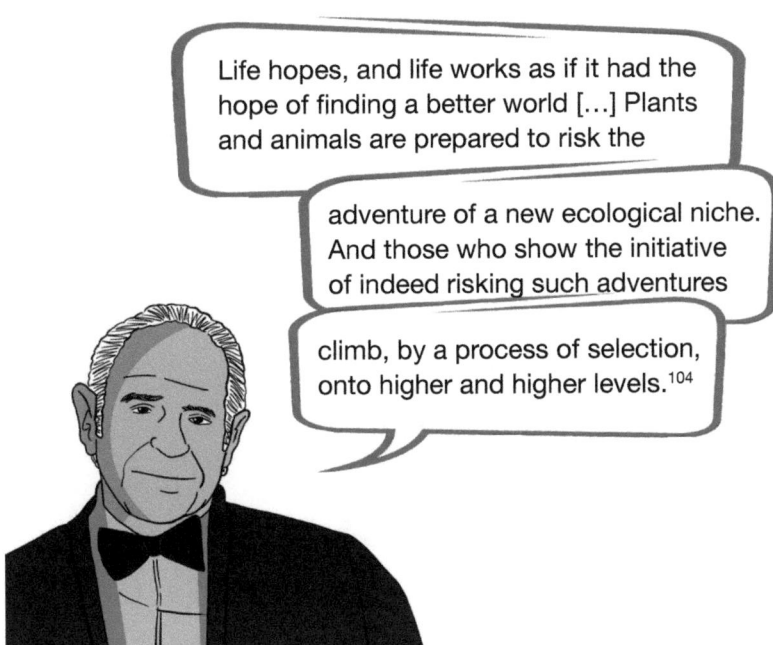

Life hopes, and life works as if it had the hope of finding a better world [...] Plants and animals are prepared to risk the adventure of a new ecological niche. And those who show the initiative of indeed risking such adventures climb, by a process of selection, onto higher and higher levels.[104]

Thus there exists, for example, a type of crab which has mastered the problem of global warming and of the increasingly longer drought spells that this warming brings with it by undergoing mutation. The eggs of this species of crab can go for up to thirty years without drying out. The larvae can thus survive very long periods of drought and emerge only when conditions of extreme dampness have returned, as for example after a flood. A mammal species, the bat, has also succeeded, by means of numerous mutations, in developing an ability to fly, so as to be able to settle in the roofs of buildings formerly inhabited by human beings. In the light of such examples, Popper comes to the conclusion:

From the very start, most likely by a process of Darwinian selection, life seeks a better world.[105]

Much the same applies to Man as applies to plants and animals:

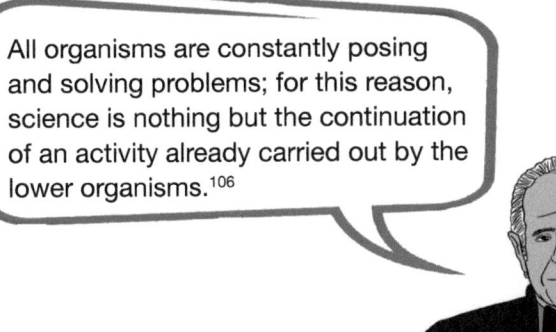

All organisms are constantly posing and solving problems; for this reason, science is nothing but the continuation of an activity already carried out by the lower organisms.[106]

Just like new mutations, new scientific hypotheses only survive if they are able to prove and assert themselves within their own external environment. Also among scientific theories, Popper argues, there is such a thing as a "struggle for survival":

The struggle for survival extends above all to theories.[107]

And there is also a 'natural selection' among theories.[108]

Only the most successful theories are retained. The process of trial and error, i.e. of the trying out of new solutions, is the same:

> From the amoeba to Einstein
> is just a single step.[109]

Common to the amoeba, Einstein, and us ourselves is the lifelong attempt to improve our situation, to solve our problems or, as Popper puts it, "to raise ourselves onto a higher level". And it is precisely in this that the meaning of our existence inheres. We must never stop trying to correct our own errors:

> The cultivation of this method of the timely
> correction of our errors is a moral duty;
> it is the duty of incessant self-criticism,
> constant learning, the duty to carry out
> constant small improvements to our
> attitude, our judgments – also our moral
> judgments – and our theories.[110]

This way of "giving meaning to one's life" recommended by Popper may sound, to many people, lacking in poetry and promise. Popper urges us, however, to remain modest and humble and to recognize that, if mankind has an essential destiny, this destiny is connected with our capacity always to develop new ideas to deal with the problems we encounter:

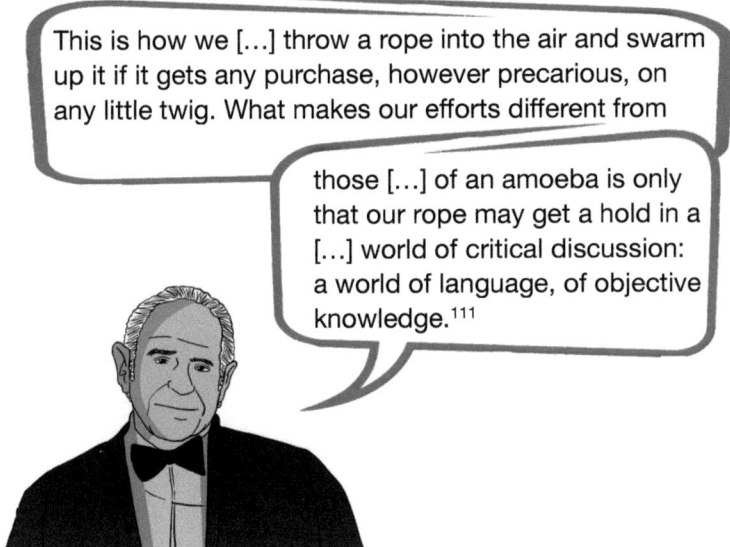

This is how we [...] throw a rope into the air and swarm up it if it gets any purchase, however precarious, on any little twig. What makes our efforts different from

those [...] of an amoeba is only that our rope may get a hold in a [...] world of critical discussion: a world of language, of objective knowledge.[111]

Bibliographical References

1   Karl Popper, The Open Society and Its Enemies, New, One-Volume
    Edition, Princeton University Press, 2013, p. 189.
2   Karl Popper, Conjectures and Refutations, Basic Books, New York and
    London, 1962, p. 33.
3   Karl Popper and Konrad Lorenz, Die Zukunft ist Offen,
    Piper Publishers, Munich 1985, p. 49.
4   Ibid.
5   Ibid. p. 50.
6   Karl Popper, The Logic of Scientific Discovery, Routledge Classics,
    London and New York, p. 4.
7   Karl Popper, The World of Parmenides, Essays on the Presocratic
    Enlightenment, Routledge, London and New York, 1998, p. 25.
8   Karl Popper in an interview with Manfred Schell for the newspaper
    "Die Welt", published in nos. 42, 44 and 46 of this newspaper in the
    year 1990. No full English translation of this three-part interview
    exists and the text of the quoted passages is the work of the translator
    of the present book. This interview is referred to several more times
    below, always as "Die Welt 1990"
9   Ibid.
10 Karl Popper, The Open Society and Its Enemies, New, One-Volume
    Edition, Princeton University Press, 2013, p. 189.
11 Karl Popper, Die Welt 1990.
12 Karl Popper, The Open Society and Its Enemies, New, One-Volume
    Edition, Princeton University Press, 2013, p. xxxix
    (Preface to Second Edition).
13 Karl Popper, Die Welt 1990.
14 Ibid.
15 Ibid.
16 Karl Popper and Konrad Lorenz, Die Zukunft ist Offen, Piper
    Publishers, Munich 1985, p. 103.
17 Karl Popper, Objective Knowledge : An Evolutionary Approach
    (Revised Edition) Clarendon Press, Oxford, 1972, p. 211
18 Karl Popper and Konrad Lorenz, Die Zukunft ist Offen, Piper
    Publishers, Munich 1985, p. 52.

19 Ibid. p. 60.
20 Karl Popper, Unended Quest, : An Intellectual Autobiography, Routledge, London and New York, 1992, pp. 38-39
21 Ibid.
22 Ibid.
23 Karl Popper and Konrad Lorenz, Die Zukunft ist Offen, Piper Publishers, Munich 1985, p. 52.
24 Karl Popper, The Logic of Scientific Discovery, Routledge Classics, London and New York, p. 4.
25 Karl Popper, Objective Knowledge : An Evolutionary Approach (Revised Edition) Clarendon Press, Oxford, 1972, p. 7
26 Karl Popper, Die Welt 1990, p. 24
27 Karl Popper and Konrad Lorenz, Die Zukunft ist Offen, Piper Publishers, Munich 1985, p. 50.
28 Ibid.
29 Ibid. p. 54.
30 Karl Popper, Die Welt 1990. p. 24.
31 Karl Popper, Objective Knowledge : An Evolutionary Approach (Revised Edition) Clarendon Press, Oxford, 1972, p. 81.
32 Karl Popper and Konrad Lorenz, Die Zukunft ist Offen, Piper Publishers, Munich 1985, p. 52.
33 Ibid. p. 135.
34 Karl Popper, The Open Society and Its Enemies, New, One-Volume Edition, Princeton University Press, 2013, p. 55.
35 Ibid. p. 164.
36 Ibid. p. 165.
37 Ibid. p. 613 (this passage appears at the end of the two-volume English edition of Popper's book as part of a note to Chapter Ten).
38 Ibid. p. xl (Preface to Second Edition).
39 Ibid.
40 Ibid. p. 189.
41 Karl Popper, The Open Society and Its Enemies, German edition, Volume 5 of the Studienausgabe, Mohr Siebeck Publishers, Tuebingen, 2003, p. xiv.
42 Ibid. p. ix.
43 Ibid.
44 Karl Popper, The Open Society and Its Enemies, New, One-Volume Edition, Princeton University Press, 2013, p. 83.

45 Ibid. p. 84.

46 Ibid. p. 150.

47 Karl Popper, Die Welt 1990. p. 93.

48 The Dialogues of Plato, translated by Benjamin Jowett, in five volumes, MacMillan and Co. New York and London, 1892 ; Volume Five : The Laws, pp. 295-6.

49 Ibid. pp. 296-7.

50 Karl Popper, Die Welt 1990. p. 47.

51 Karl Popper and Konrad Lorenz, Die Zukunft ist Offen, Piper Publishers, Munich 1985, p. 139.

52 Karl Popper, The Open Society and Its Enemies, New, One-Volume Edition, Princeton University Press, 2013, p. 115.

53 Karl Popper and Konrad Lorenz, Die Zukunft ist Offen, Piper Publishers, Munich 1985, p. 110.

54 Ibid. p. 140.

55 Ibid. p. 105.

56 Karl Popper, The Open Society and Its Enemies, New, One-Volume Edition, Princeton University Press, 2013, p. 246.

57 Ibid. p. 277.

58 Ibid. p. 273.

59 Karl Popper, Die Welt 1990. p. 98.

60 Ibid. p. 100.

61 Ibid. p. 55.

62 Karl Popper, The Open Society and Its Enemies, New, One-Volume Edition, Princeton University Press, 2013, pp. 474-75.

63 Karl Popper, Preface to The Poverty of Historicism. The passage in fact appears only in the Preface to the 1965 German edition : Das Elend des Historismus, published by J.C.B. Mohr in Tuebingen, Germany in 1965, p. viii.

64 Karl Popper, Die Welt 1990. p. 98.

65 Karl Popper, The Poverty of Historicism, Harper Torchbooks, Harper and Row, New York and Evanston, 1964, p. vii (Preface).

66 Karl Popper, Objective Knowledge : An Evolutionary Approach (Revised Edition) Clarendon Press, Oxford, 1972, p. 81.

67 Karl Popper and Konrad Lorenz, Die Zukunft ist Offen, Piper Publishers, Munich 1985, p. 109.

68 Karl Popper, The Open Society and Its Enemies, New, One-Volume Edition, Princeton University Press, 2013, pp. 431.

69 Karl Popper, Die Welt 1990. p. 18.

70 Karl Popper, The Poverty of Historicism, Harper Torchbooks, Harper and Row, New York and Evanston, 1964, p. 66.

71 Karl Popper and Konrad Lorenz, Die Zukunft ist Offen, Piper Publishers, Munich 1985, p. 138.

72 In the years 1975 and 1976 there appeared two books with the title Critical Rationalism and Social Democracy. Helmut Schmidt himself wrote the preface to them. Although he does not, in this preface, "officially" declare himself a Critical Rationalist, he certainly does advocate here a basic attitude of (self-)critique and a policy of gradual reform rather than the pursuit of a socially revolutionary utopia. See Kritischer Rationalismus und Sozialdemokratie, edited by Georg Luehrs, Thilo Sarrazin and Frithjof Speer, J. H. W. Dietz Publishers, Bonn, 1982.

73 Karl Popper and Konrad Lorenz, Die Zukunft ist Offen, Piper Publishers, Munich 1985, p. 134.

74 Karl Popper, Die Welt 1990. p. 95.

75 Ibid.

76 Ibid. p. 92.

77 Ibid. p. 93.

78 Ibid.

79 Considerable criticism was directed at the alleged lack of care with which Popper had examined Plato's, Hegel's and Marx's actual texts. Thus, Henning Ottmann writes of 'The Open Society and Its Enemies': "As far as the interpretation of the authors criticized is concerned the two volumes are one long hermeneutic catastrophe [...] a "chamber of horrors" of the history of ideas. Popper was simply not intellectually equipped for the task of historical-hermeneutic interpretation. If one wishes to make anything of the book at all, then one must take it as a theory of Popper's own politics presented in historical disguise. In this respect it is highly revealing." Henning Ottmann, Geschichte des Politischen Denkens, Das 20te Jahrhundert von der Kritischen Theorie bis zur Globalisierung, Metzler Publishers, Stuttgart, 2012, p. 137 ff.

80 G.W.F. Hegel, The Phenomenology of Spirit, Cambridge University Press, 2018, p. 18. The full text reads: "In any spirit that stands higher than another, the lower concrete existence has descended to the status of an insignificant moment; what was formerly at stake is now only a trace; its shape has been covered over and has become a simple shading of itself."

81 Ibid. p. 13.
82 Karl Popper, interview with L'Express from 1982.
83 G. W. F. Hegel, Philosophy of Right, Cambridge University Press, 1991, p. 240
84 Karl Popper and Konrad Lorenz, Die Zukunft ist Offen, Piper Publishers, Munich 1985, p. 21.
85 Ibid. p. 53.
86 Ibid. p. 106.
87 Karl Popper, The Open Society and Its Enemies, New, One-Volume Edition, Princeton University Press, 2013, p. 294.
88 Ibid. p. 442.
89 Karl Popper, Die Welt 1990. p. 88.
90 Karl Popper, The Open Society and Its Enemies, New, One-Volume Edition, Princeton University Press, 2013, p. xliii (Introduction)
91 Karl Popper, The Logic of the Social Sciences, in Adorno, Popper et al, The Positivist Dispute in German Sociology, Heinemann Books, London 1976, p. 89
92 Ibid.
93 See the interview given by Popper in 1971 to the German weekly newspaper "Die Zeit", entitled "Against Big Words". It is here that Popper describes in particular the language adopted by Adorno and Habermas in their sociological writings, a language full of foreign terms and elaborate sub-clauses, as "obscurantism" of the sort that he had already criticized in Hegel. He attempts to demonstrate the "sub stancelessness" by simplifying certain passages of the texts that these two writers had published in the course of the "Positivism Dispute". Adorno and Habermas, Popper here claims, deliberately express them selves in this extremely complicated way so as to make themselves immune to criticism. But it is the duty of a man of science, he goes on, vis-à-vis the open society that he lives in to formulate his theories in such a way that they are comprehensible and criticisable.
94 Theodor Adorno, On the Logic of the Social Sciences, in Adorno, Popper et al, The Positivist Dispute in German Sociology, Heinemann Books, London 1976, p. 114.
95 Karl Popper, The Logic of Scientific Discovery, Routledge Classics, London and New York, p. 18.

96 Karl Popper, in Franz Stark (ed.) Revolution oder Reform ? Herbert Marcuse und Karl Popper : Eine Konfrontation, Koesel Verlag, Munich, 1971, p. 37 f.

97 Karl Popper, The Logic of Scientific Discovery, Routledge Classics, London and New York, p. 22.

98 Karl Popper, All Life is Problem-Solving, Routledge, London and New York, 2001.

99 Karl Popper and Konrad Lorenz, Die Zukunft ist Offen, Piper Publishers, Munich 1985, p. 131.

100 From Karl Popper, Freiheit und Intellektuelle Verantwortung, Politische Aufsaetze und Vortraege aus Sechs Jahrzehnten, p. 333 of Volume 14 of the German Collected Works.

101 Karl Popper, Die Welt 1990. p. 78.

102 Karl Popper and Konrad Lorenz, Die Zukunft ist Offen, Piper Publishers, Munich 1985, p. 42.

103 Karl Popper, Die Welt 1990. p. 24.

104 Karl Popper and Konrad Lorenz, Die Zukunft ist Offen, Piper Publishers, Munich 1985, p. 21.

105 Ibid.

106 Ibid. p. 53.

107 Ibid. p. 60.

108 Ibid. p. 54.

109 Ibid. p. 53.

110 Karl Popper, Preface to The Poverty of Historicism. The passage in fact appears only in the Preface to the 1965 German edition : Das Elend des Historismus, published by J.C.B. Mohr in Tuebingen, Germany in 1965 (p.ix).

111 Karl Popper, Objective Knowledge : An Evolutionary Approach (Revised Edition) Clarendon Press, Oxford, 1972, p. 148.

Already published in the same series:

Walther Ziegler
Camus in 60 Minutes
ISBN 9783741227738

Walther Ziegler
Freud in 60 Minutes
ISBN 9783741227707

Walther Ziegler
Hegel in 60 Minutes
ISBN 9783741227677

Walther Ziegler
Heidegger in 60 Minutes
ISBN 9783741227752

Walther Ziegler
Kant in 60 Minutes
ISBN 9783741226373

Walther Ziegler
Marx in 60 Minutes
ISBN 9783741227691

Walther Ziegler
Nietzsche in 60 Minutes
ISBN 9783752803822

Walther Ziegler
Platon in 60 Minutes
ISBN 9783741227615

Walther Ziegler
Sartre in 60 Minutes
ISBN 9783741227653

Walther Ziegler
Rousseau in 60 Minutes
ISBN 9783741227622

Walther Ziegler
Smith in 60 Minutes
ISBN 9783741227721

Walther Ziegler
Rawls in 60 Minutes
ISBN 9783750424050

Walther Ziegler
Wittgenstein in 60 Minutes

Walther Ziegler
Adorno in 60 Minutes

Walther Ziegler
Hobbes in 60 Minutes

Walther Ziegler
Popper in 60 Minutes

Coming soon in the same series:

Walther Ziegler
Arendt in 60 Minutes

Walther Ziegler
Foucault in 60 Minutes

Walther Ziegler
Habermas in 60 Minutes

Walther Ziegler
Schopenhauer in 60 Minutes

The author:

Dr Walther Ziegler is academically trained in the fields of philosophy, history and political science. As a foreign correspondent, reporter and newsroom coordinator for the German TV station ProSieben he has produced films on every continent. His news reports have won several prizes and awards.He has also authored numerous books in the field of philosophy. His many years of experience as a journalist mean that he is able to present the complex ideas of the great philosophers in a way that is both engaging and very clear. Since 2007 he has also been active as a teacher and trainer of young TV journalists in Munich, holding the post of Academic Director at the Media Academy, an institute of higher education that offers film and TV courses at its base directly on the site of the major European film production company Bavaria Film.